Human Rights of Migrants in the 21st Century

This book offers an accessible examination of the human rights of migrants in the context of the UN's negotiations in 2018.

This volume has two main contributions. Firstly, it is designed to inform the negotiations on the UN's Global Compact for Safe, Orderly and Regular Migration announced by the New York Declaration of the UN General Assembly on 19 September 2016. Second, it intends to assist officials, lawyers and academics to ensure that the human rights of migrants are fully respected by state authorities and international organisations and safeguarded by national and supranational courts across the globe. The overall objective of this book is to clarify problem areas which migrants encounter as non-citizens of the state where they are and how international human rights obligations of those states provide solutions. It defines the existing international human rights of migrants and provides the source of States' obligations. In order to provide a clear and useful guide to the existing human rights of migrants, the volume examines these rights from the perspective of the migrant: what situations do people encounter as their status changes from citizen (in their own country) to migrant (in a foreign state), and how do human rights provide legal entitlements regarding their treatment by a foreign state?

This book will be of much interest to students of migration, human rights, international law and international relations.

Elspeth Guild is Jean Monnet Professor ad personam, Queen Mary University of London, UK.

Stefanie Grant is Senior Visiting Fellow, Centre for the Study of Human Rights, London School of Economics, UK.

C. A. Groenendijk is Emeritus Professor of Sociology of Law, Radboud University, Netherlands.

Routledge Studies in Liberty and Security

Series editors: Didier Bigo
Elspeth Guild and R.B.J. Walker

This book series will establish connections between critical security studies and international relations, surveillance studies, criminology, law and human rights, political sociology and political theory. To analyse the boundaries of the concepts of liberty and security, the practices which are enacted in their name (often the same practices) will be at the heart of the series. These investigations address contemporary questions informed by history, political theory and a sense of what constitutes the contemporary international order.

Justice and Security in the 21st Century
Risks, Rights and the Rule of Law
Synnøve Ugelvik and Barbara Hudson

Transnational Power Elites
The New Professionals of Governance, Law and Security
Edited by Niilo Kauppi and Mikael Rask Madsen

Security and Defensive Democracy in Israel
A Critical Approach to Political Discourse
Sharon Weinblum

Managing State Fragility
Conflict, Quantification, and Power
Isabel Rocha de Siqueira

Governing Diasporas in International Relations
The Transnational Politics of Croatia and Former Yugoslavia
Francesco Ragazzi

Human Rights of Migrants in the 21st Century
Edited by Elspeth Guild, Stefanie Grant and C. A. Groenendijk

Human Rights of Migrants in the 21st Century

**Edited by Elspeth Guild,
Stefanie Grant and
C. A. Groenendijk**

Routledge
Taylor & Francis Group

LONDON AND NEW YORK

First published 2018
by Routledge
2 Park Square, Milton Park, Abingdon, Oxon OX14 4RN

and by Routledge
711 Third Avenue, New York, NY 10017

Routledge is an imprint of the Taylor & Francis Group, an informa business

British Library Cataloguing-in-Publication Data
A catalogue record for this book is available from the British Library

Library of Congress Cataloging-in-Publication Data
Names: Guild, Elspeth, editor. | Grant, Stefanie, editor. |
    Groenendijk, C. A., editor.
Title: Human rights of migrants in the 21st century / edited by
    Elspeth Guild, Stefanie Grant and C.A. Groenendijk.
Other titles: Human rights of migrants in the twenty-first century
Description: Abingdon, Oxon ; New York, NY : Routledge, 2018. |
    Series: Routledge studies in liberty and security | Includes
    bibliographical references and index.
Identifiers: LCCN 2017025317 | ISBN 9781138503397 (hardback) |
    ISBN 9781315145396 (ebook)
Subjects: LCSH: Respect for persons—Law and legislation. |
    Human rights. | Emigration and immigration law. |
    Discrimination—Law and legislation. | International law.
Classification: LCC K3249 .H85 2018 | DDC 342.08/2—dc23
LC record available at https://lccn.loc.gov/2017025317

ISBN: 978-1-138-50339-7 (hbk)
ISBN: 978-1-315-14539-6 (ebk)

Typeset in Times New Roman
by Apex CoVantage, LLC

Contents

List of abbreviations   ix
List of contributors   xii

1 **Introduction**   1
ELSPETH GUILD, STEFANIE GRANT AND C. A. GROENENDIJK

2 **The right to be recognised as a person before the law**   16
KATHRYN ALLINSON

3 **Migrants' rights at the border**   21
CEREN MUTUS TOPRAKSEVEN

4 **Immigration detention**   27
KATHRYN ALLINSON, JUSTINE STEFANELLI AND
KATHARINE T. WEATHERHEAD

5 **Irregular status**   35
KATHARINE T. WEATHERHEAD

6 **Rights of residence, termination of residence and
in respect of removal**   42
VALERIA VITA

7 **The economic, social and cultural rights of migrants**   50
CLAUDE CAHN

8 **Rights at work**   58
BJARNEY FRIÐRIKSDÓTTIR

 9 **Family life and the migrant**   67
    ROWENA MOFFATT, ELLA GUNN AND ANUSCHEH FARAHAT

10 **Freedom of thought, belief and religion and freedom
    of expression and opinion**   72
    SUSIE ALEGRE

11 **The right to an effective remedy, the right to an
    effective national procedure against arbitrary
    removal and the right to a fair hearing**   78
    DANA BALDINGER

12 **Conclusion and summary of key international
    human rights of migrants**   85
    ELSPETH GUILD, STEFANIE GRANT AND C. A. GROENENDIJK

    Bibliography   91
    Index   93

Abbreviations

Body of Principles:	UN General Assembly, Body of Principles for the Protection of All Persons under Any Form of Detention or Imprisonment (Body of Principles) (9 December 1988, A/RES/43/173)
CEDAW:	Convention on the Elimination of All Forms of Discrimination against Women 1981
CEDAW Committee:	The Treaty Body that monitors implementation of CEDAW by its State parties
CERD Committee:	UN Committee on the Elimination of Racial Discrimination (the Treaty Body that monitors implementation of the ICERD by its State parties)
Child Rights Convention:	UN Convention on the Rights of the Child 1989
Civil and Political Rights Covenant:	International Covenant on Civil and Political Rights 1966
Committee against Torture:	The Treaty Body that monitors implementation of the Convention against Torture by its State parties
Committee on the Elimination of Discrimination Against Women:	The Treaty Body that monitors implementation of the Convention on the Elimination of All Forms of Discrimination against Women by its State parties

Committee on the Rights of the Child:	The Treaty Body that monitors implementation of the Child Rights Convention by its State parties
Convention against Torture:	Convention against Torture and Other Cruel, Inhuman or Degrading Treatment or Punishment 1994
Convention on the Rights of Persons with Disabilities:	UN Convention on the Rights of Persons with Disabilities 2006
Global Compact on Migration:	UN Global Compact for Safe, Orderly and Regular Migration
Human Rights Committee:	The Treaty Body that monitors implementation of the International Covenant on Civil and Political Rights by its State parties
Human Rights Council:	The intergovernmental body within the United Nations system responsible for strengthening the promotion and protection of human rights
ICERD:	International Convention on the Elimination of All Forms of Racial Discrimination 1965
ILO:	International Labour Organization
Migrant Workers Committee:	The Treaty Body that monitors implementation of the Migrant Workers Convention by its State parties
Migrant Workers Convention:	International Convention on the Protection of the Rights of All Migrant Workers and Members of Their Families 1990
New York Declaration:	The New York Declaration for Refugees and Migrants adopted by the General Assembly on 19 September 2016
OHCHR:	Office of the UN High Commissioner for Human Rights
Refugee Convention:	Convention Relating to the Status of Refugees 1951 and its 1967 Protocol
Social Rights Committee:	UN Committee on Economic, Social and Cultural Rights 1966 (the Treaty Body that monitors implementation of the Social Rights Convention by its State parties)

Social Rights Covenant:	International Covenant on Economic, Social and Cultural Rights 1966
The Universal Declaration:	The Universal Declaration of Human Rights 1948.
UN:	United Nations
UNHCR:	United Nations High Commissioner for Refugees
UNHCR Guidelines on Detention:	UNHCR Guidelines on the applicable criteria and standards relating to the detention of asylum seekers and alternatives to detention 2012
Working Group on Enforced or Involuntary Disappearances:	Mandated by the Human Rights Council to assist families in determining the fate or whereabouts of their family members who are reportedly disappeared

Contributors

Susie Alegre is a barrister at Doughty Street Chambers, London. She also holds the position of Interception of Communications Commissioner for the Isle of Man and is an associate at the Policy Practice. She has particular expertise in accountability and oversight mechanisms in different jurisdictions including co-chairing the Donor Accountability Working Group on corruption in Uganda on behalf of the EU from 2010–2013, and previously served as ombudsman for the UK Financial Ombudsman Service where she specialised in complex cases involving equality and European consumer law. She previously held the post of anti-terrorism adviser to the Organization for Security and Co-operation in Europe Office for Democratic Institutions and Human Rights. In this role, she developed technical assistance projects, including a training programme and manual for government officials on human rights in the fight against terrorism.

Kathryn Allinson is a PhD candidate at Queen Mary, University of London (QMUL). She holds an LLM in international human rights law (QMUL), a GDL (BPP Law School) and a BA in politics with philosophy (Durham University). During her LLM program, Kathryn was awarded the QM Postgraduate Essay Competition in Migration Law prize for an essay on State accountability for causing refugees flows during the War on Terror campaigns in Iraq and Afghanistan. She has previously worked in the non-governmental organization (NGO) sector for legal-action charity, Reprieve, an international development organisation; WaterAid; and in Rwanda with local human rights organisations on programme design. Her PhD research examines state responsibility in the context of accountability for forced migration flows.

Dana Baldinger is Vice-president of the District Court of Amsterdam. She holds a PhD from Amsterdam/Nijmegen and has worked in the field of asylum law, criminal law and juvenile law. She has published various articles on judicial scrutiny in asylum cases and is the author of *Vertical Judicial Dialogues in Asylum Cases Standards on Judicial Scrutiny and Evidence in International and European Asylum Law* (Brill/Martinus Nijhoff, 2015) and *Rigorous Scrutiny Versus Marginal Review: Standards on Judicial Scrutiny and Evidence in International and European Asylum Law* (Wolf Legal Publishers 2013).

Claude Cahn is human rights adviser, Office of the High Commissioner for Human Rights (OHCHR), based in the Office of the United Nations Resident Coordinator in Serbia. He has over 20 years of professional human rights, equality and social justice experience. He previously held the post of human rights adviser (OHCHR) in Moldova and worked at the European Roma Rights Centre, as well as at the Centre on Housing Rights and Evictions. He holds a PhD in law from Radboud University Nijmegen. He is the author *of Human Rights, State Sovereignty and Medical Ethics* (Brill/Martinus Nijhoff, 2014) and the editor of *Roma Rights: Race, Justice and Strategies for Equality* (International Debate Education Association 2002).

Anuscheh Farahat is a senior research affiliate at the Max Planck Institute for Comparative Public Law and International Law (Heidelberg, Germany). She leads an Emmy-Noether Research Group at Goethe University (Frankfurt), which examines the role of constitutional courts in transnational solidarity conflicts. She holds an LLM (Berkeley) and a PhD (Goethe University). In 2014, her PhD thesis *Progressive Inclusion: Migrant Citizenship and Transnational Migration* was published by Springer, and it has received multiple awards including the Herman-Mosler-Preis 2015 of the German Society of International Law.

Bjarney Friðriksdóttir is a researcher at Radboud University, Nijmegen Netherlands. In November 2016, she was awarded a PhD in law from Radboud. She also holds an MA in international affairs from Columbia University, New York, and an MA in public international law from the University of Amsterdam. Her experience includes working as a senior adviser on trafficking in human beings for the Council of the Baltic Sea States and working with international organisations in the field for several years, including as a protection officer with the United Nations High Commissioner for Refugees in Syria and as the international manager of the United Nations Development Fund for Women Project Office in Kosovo. From 1997–2001, she was the director of the Icelandic Human Rights Centre and from 2001–2003 the director of the Intercultural Centre in Reykjavik.

Stefanie Grant is a visiting senior fellow at the Centre for the Study of Human Rights at the London School of Economics. Her current work is on irregular cross-border journeys, identification of those who die and the rights of their families. She has headed Amnesty International's Research Department in London, represented Amnesty in Washington DC, acted for immigrants and refugees as a solicitor in London, directed the research branch of the UN's OHCHR in Geneva and consulted for other intergovernmental organisations. She is chair of the Institute on Statelessness and Inclusion.

C. A. Groenendijk is emeritus professor of sociology of law at the Faculty of Law, Radboud University, Netherlands, and founder and research fellow of its Centre for Migration Law. He was chairman of the Standing Committee of Experts on international immigration, refugee and criminal law (1997–2014). He published on a number of topics including the social and legal status of immigrants in the Netherlands and the EU, immigration and race relations legislation, integration of immigrants and nationality law.

Elspeth Guild is Jean Monnet Professor ad personam at QMUL and the Radboud University Nijmegen, Netherlands. She is a partner at Kingsley Napley (a law firm in London); an associate senior research fellow at the Centre for European Policy Studies, Brussels; and a visiting Professor at the College of Europe, Bruges. Professor Guild provides regular advice to the European Parliament, the European Commission, the Council of Europe and other European and international organisations (such as the UNHCR) on free movement of persons, migration and asylum. She is co-editor of the *European Journal of Migration and Law*, and is on the editorial board of the journal *International Political Sociology*. She is co-editor of the book series *Immigration and Asylum Law and Policy in Europe* published by Martinus Nijhoff.

Ella Gunn is a legal researcher at Garden Court Chambers, London. She is an Australian qualified solicitor with practice experience who holds an MSc in Refugee and Forced Migration Studies from the University of Oxford and an LLB with First Class Hons from Queensland University of Technology. Her MSc dissertation received a distinction and was published as working paper by the Refugee Studies Centre, University of Oxford in 2015. She has published case notes in the *Journal of Immigration, Asylum and Nationality Law* and has acted in the role of legal editor for the Oxford Monitor of Forced Migration (OxMo).

Rowena Moffatt is a barrister at Doughty Street Chambers, London. She specialises in immigration and asylum law with a particular expertise in EU cases. She is the co-author of *EU Law in Judicial Review* (Oxford

University Press 2014) and co-editor of *The Law and Practice of Expulsion and Exclusion from the United Kingdom: Deportation, Removal, Exclusion and Denial or Deprivation of Citizenship* (Hart 2014). In 2015, Rowena earned a DPhil in Law from the University of Oxford. She convenes the Courts and Tribunals Working Group of the Immigration Law Practitioners' Association; is case notes editor of the *Journal of Immigration, Asylum and Nationality Law*; and writes practice notes for Lexis Nexis.

Justine Stefanelli is an associate senior research fellow at the Bingham Centre for the Rule of Law, London, where she conducts research primarily in European immigration and asylum law. She is also a PhD candidate at QMUL, in which she is examining the role of judicial review in safeguarding the liberty of immigration detainees in the US and the UK. She holds an LLM in European Law from Queen Mary University of London and a JD from the University of Pittsburgh, Pennsylvania (US), where she is a licensed attorney.

Ceren Mutus Toprakseven is a PhD candidate at QMUL. She holds an LLM in public international law from King's College London and an LLB from Koc University, Istanbul, and is a registered lawyer with the Istanbul Bar Association. She worked for eight years as a legal researcher at the International Strategic Research Organisation (USAK), Center for European Union Studies. Ceren's PhD research examines shared responsibility in the context of extraterritorialised or privatised migration controls.

Valeria Vita is a PhD candidate at the University of Palermo, Italy. She holds a master's degree in law from the University of Rome, Tor Vergata, and passed the bar examination in 2015. She has previously worked in the NGO sector as a legal advisor in immigration and asylum law, and she is a member of the Italian association the Association for Juridical Studies on Immigration. Her research project investigates the practice of detention and return policies for migrants in the Italian context and their impact on personal liberty. In 2016, she was a visiting research fellow at QMUL.

Katharine T. Weatherhead is a PhD candidate at QMUL. She holds an MA (Hons) in international relations and law from the University of Edinburgh and an MSc in refugee and forced migration studies from the University of Oxford. She was placed on the dean's honour list for outstanding academic achievement during an Erasmus exchange at Sciences Po Paris, and she was awarded the DP Heatley prize for excellence in politics and international relations at the University of Edinburgh.

Katharine's PhD research, which crosses the disciplines of law and international relations, and examines the creation of legal knowledge among migrants at migration transit points in the European Union.

Consulting experts

Pieter Boeles is emeritus professor of migration law at the University of Leiden and visiting professor at VU University, Amsterdam. He is the co-author of *European Migration Law* (Intersentia 2014 (2nd ed)).

Sergio Carrera is a senior research fellow and head of the Justice and the Home Affairs Unit at the Centre for European Policy Studies. He is a visiting professor at the Paris School of International Affairs at Sciences Po (France), associate professor and senior research fellow at the Faculty of Law in Maastricht University (the Netherlands) and honorary industry professor and senior research fellow at the School of Law in Queen Mary University of London (UK). He holds a PhD from Maastricht University (the Netherlands). He is the author of many articles and co-author of a number of books including *European Citizenship at the Crossroads: The Role of the European Union in Acquisition and Loss of Nationality* (Wolf Legal Publishers 2015).

Ryszard Cholewinski is a senior fellow at the Global Migration Centre based at the Graduate Institute Geneva and a migration policy specialist in the Labour Migration Branch the Conditions of Work and Equality Department at the International Labour Organisation (ILO). Prior to joining the ILO, he was a senior migration policy and research specialist at the International Organisation for Migration and Reader in Law at the University of Leicester (UK). He is the author of *Migrant Workers in International Human Rights Law: Their Protection in Countries of Employment* (Clarendon Press 1997) and two publications for the Council of Europe: *The Legal Status of Migrants Admitted for Employment* (2004) and *Irregular migrants: access to minimum social rights* (2005). He holds a PhD from the University of Ottawa, an LLM from the University of Saskatchewan and an LLB from the University of Leicester.

Mariagiulia Giuffré is a lecturer in law at Edge Hill University (UK) and a research fellow at the School of Advanced Study, University of London working on a project on externalisation of migration controls and her forthcoming monograph *The Readmission of Asylum Seekers under International Law* (Hart Publishing, Oxford). She has been recently consulted as a legal analyst by Oxford Analytica, conducting research on the law and practice of Search and Rescue in the Central Mediterranean. In

2015, Mariagiulia was a visiting research fellow at the Refugee Studies Centre, University of Oxford while – from 2010 to 2013 – she was affiliated to the Faculty of Law, Lund University (Sweden). Mariagiulia holds a PhD from the University of Trento (Italy). She has published several articles and co-authored the book *Exploring the Boundaries of Refugee Law: Current Protection Challenges* (Brill 2015).

Bethany Hastie is a lecturer at Allard School of Law, the University of British Columbia, Canada. Dr. Hastie completed her doctorate in law at McGill University in 2015. During her tenure at McGill, she was an O'Brien Fellow in Human Rights and Legal Pluralism, a doctoral fellow with the Social Sciences and Humanities Research Council of Canada, the Ian C Pilarczyk Teaching Fellow in Legal Research Methodology and a research member with the Oppenheimer Chair of Public International Law and the Institute of Comparative Law. She has worked with a variety of organisations on projects related to her research including the Canadian Council for Refugees, the BC Office to Combat Trafficking in Persons and the European Commission against Racism and Intolerance.

Pia Oberoi is an advisor on migration and human rights at the UN OHCHR (Geneva) where she leads the work of OHCHR's migration team on policy and legal issues. Prior to this, she worked as human rights officer at the OHCHR and as a refugee and migrants rights officer at Amnesty International. Pia holds a DPhil in international relations from the University of Oxford.

Helena Wray is an associate professor of law at the University of Exeter and an associate professor in law at Middlesex University. She is the author of *Regulating Marriage Migration into the UK: A Stranger in the Home* (Ashgate 2011) and contributing author for the *Textbook on Immigration and Asylum Law* (Oxford University Press 2014). She is an executive committee member of the Migration and Law Network and has authored or co-authored several policy submissions on behalf of the Network. She is the editor of the *Journal of Immigration, Asylum and Nationality Law*.

1   Introduction

Elspeth Guild, Stefanie Grant
and C. A. Groenendijk

*We reaffirm the purposes and principles of the Charter of the United
Nations. We reaffirm also the Universal Declaration of Human Rights and
recall the core international human rights treaties. We reaffirm and will
fully protect the human rights of all refugees and migrants, regardless of
status; all are rights holders.*
New York Declaration of the UN General Assembly
19 September 2016[1]

For the first time in its history, the UN adopted a Declaration for Migrants
and Refugees[2] on 19 September 2016 which calls for two Global Compacts:[3]
one for safe, orderly and regular migration and the other for refugees. The
context of the New York Declaration is the ongoing large movements of
migrants and refugees, and the objective to achieve international agreement
on commitments to both safe, orderly and regular migration and refugees.
It contains three types of commitments – those relevant to migrants and
refugees, those specific to migrants and those relevant only to refugees.
The commitments to both migrants and refugees are to "people-centred,
sensitive, humane, dignified, gender-responsive and prompt reception for
all persons arriving in our countries".[4] The international community's commitment to migrants is "protecting the safety, dignity and human rights and
fundamental freedoms of all migrants, regardless of their migratory status,
at all times"[5] and to refugees to address the issues which force people to
flee – to "work to address the root causes of such crisis situations and to
prevent or resolve conflict by peaceful means."[6] Migration, both voluntary
and forced (that is of refugees) is a matter of substantial tension in the international community. Put simply, one country's migrant is another country's
citizen. Thus the interests of States are not always in alignment regarding
how someone who is simultaneously a migrant in the state where he or she
is currently and a citizen of his or her home country with an entitlement to
consular protection by that state. Refugee flight can be even more sensitive

for the international community where providing refuge to someone can be seen as a criticism of his or her state of origin. This is particularly the case where the individual seeks asylum on the ground that his or her country of origin is persecuting him or her.

Addressing these tensions is at the heart of the New York Declaration and a courageous step towards resolving them. The New York Declaration provides a particularly strong starting point for the two Compacts – it requires the Compacts to start from the existing international human rights commitments of States arising from the Universal Declaration and the human rights conventions to which States have committed themselves. For refugees, this direction is straightforward as the international community can start from the Refugee Convention which sets out a clear floor of rights for refugees and has a strong international organisation, UNHCR, which is responsible for ensuring protection of refugees. Migrants are not so fortunate. There is one UN convention relating specifically to them, but it is a fairly young convention and still needs to be ratified by many States (which the Declaration calls for). There is no one international organisation which is clearly and unambiguously responsible for migrants in particular as regards the protection of their human rights.[7] Instead, migrants' entitlement to human rights comes from the application of UN human rights conventions to 'everyone' – citizens, aliens, everyone. It is the objective of this book to bring together these human rights from the perspective of the migrants who need to rely on them.

The New York Declaration is particularly clear that the international community wishes that the starting place of the Compacts be the existing human rights of refugees and migrants. To facilitate that objective, it is necessary then to set out what those rights are. In order to do so, we primarily use two sources of international law: first the UN conventions themselves and secondly the General Comments of the Treaty Bodies established to ensure correct State compliance with the obligations. Occasionally, we also make reference to established legal opinion and Opinions of Treaty Bodies in particular cases. There is a wealth of regional standard setting both in the area of refugees and migrants. As the purpose of this book is to clarify the existing human rights of migrants at the international level, we have not used this regional material, which commits only States in the relevant geographical area. While regional standards are very important to the development of consensus on human rights at the UN level, for our purposes, we only include clearly demonstrated legal consensus on the human rights of migrants at the international level through the UN bodies. Further, many UN bodies have produced excellent and detailed work on the human rights of migrants. However, there is a need for an overview which is legally sound, reliable and available to everyone, not just the specialist reader. This is what we aim to do here.

To achieve our objective, we have structured this book around the problems and issues which migrants encounter with State authorities and address the problems from the perspective of existing and binding international human rights law. This is somewhat different from the normal legal textbook approach which starts with the law and then applies it. Instead, we start from the problem and then elucidate it from the perspective of human rights law. To make each issue clear and accessible, at the start of each chapter a specific problem encountered by a migrant which has been addressed in an Opinion of a Treaty Body on the compatibility of the State authorities' action with its human rights obligations is included.[8] We have included reference to the opinion in each case, which reveals the State in respect of the which the matter arose. But this is not intended as an exercise in highlighting shortcomings in specific countries. It is the by-product of our commitment to accuracy and accountability. In these times of allegations of fake news, we take very seriously our obligation of complete transparency.

Migrants have human rights:[9] this is a legal fact in international, regional and national law around the world.[10] As human beings, migrants are entitled to the protection and guarantee of human rights by all States within whose jurisdiction they may find themselves. Human rights are not exclusively for citizens; they are for everyone. Respect for the human rights of migrants is not aspirational or optional, but obligatory for State authorities. National law must conform to those international obligations to which States have committed themselves. These commitments have been drafted, negotiated and adopted by States themselves; they are not 'imposed' on them by some outside entity. Of particular importance for migrants are States' international human rights commitments, which constitute a floor of rights below which national law and the actions of State authorities must not fall. State officials must act in conformity with national, regional and international law, including human rights law, in all their activities regarding migrants, be they at the borders, within the State or simply under their jurisdiction.

All State authorities must apply their State's international human rights commitments in their daily work. As the Human Rights Committee has clarified in General Comment 31 regarding the Civil and Political Rights Covenant but equally relevant to all States' human rights commitments:

> 4 All branches of government (executive, legislative and judicial), and other public or governmental authorities, at whatever level – national, regional or local – are in a position to engage the responsibility of the State Party. The executive branch that usually represents the State Party internationally, including before the Committee, may not point to the fact that an action incompatible with

the provisions of the Covenant was carried out by another branch of government as a means of seeking to relieve the State Party from responsibility for the action and consequent incompatibility.[11]

This reality might have been controversial 40 years ago, but today, UN institutions and their regional counterparts are increasingly engaged in the protection of human rights of people by States of which they are not citizens (often classified as foreigners, aliens, migrants, immigrants, etc., but consistent with the approach of OHCHR, we use the term migrant). As a matter of fact, the Human Rights Committee's experience in examining State reports shows that rights that migrants should enjoy under the Civil and Political Rights Covenant are denied to them or are subject to limitations that cannot always be justified under it.[12] The description of a person as a migrant is not a justification for State action which is incompatible with UN and regional human rights obligations. International human rights law is the creation of States, to which States have voluntarily bound themselves through their ratification of the conventions. All States have a strong interest in ensuring that they comply with their international human rights obligations. Migration is no exception, but it is a field where tensions arise.

As the Human Rights Committee has clarified in General Comment 31:

> 2   While article 2[13] is couched in terms of the obligations of State Parties towards individuals as the right-holders under the Covenant, every State Party has a legal interest in the performance by every other State Party of its obligations. This follows from the fact that the 'rules concerning the basic rights of the human person' are *erga omnes* obligations and that, as indicated in the fourth preambular paragraph of the Covenant, there is a United Nations Charter obligation to promote universal respect for, and observance of, human rights and fundamental freedoms. Furthermore, the contractual dimension of the treaty involves any State Party to a treaty being obligated to every other State Party to comply with its undertakings under the treaty.

It is not only a duty of States to comply with their human rights obligations; it is in their interest and that of every State party to human rights conventions. These duties are a central part of the international relations system established under the UN.

The objective of this book is to clarify problem areas which migrants encounter as non-citizens of the State where they are and how international human rights of those States provide solutions. It defines the existing international human rights of migrants and provides the source of States' obligations. In order to provide a clear and useful guide to the existing human rights of migrants, we have chosen to examine these rights from the perspective of the migrant: what situations do people encounter as their status changes from citizen (in their own country) to migrant (in a foreign State), and how do human rights provide legal entitlements regarding their treatment by a foreign State?

Purpose and scope

This book is designed first to inform the negotiations on the UN's Global Compact for Safe, Orderly and Regular Migration (the Global Compact on Migration) announced by the New York Declaration of the UN General Assembly on 19 September 2016.[14] Many of the rights which we address here are equally relevant for refugees and people seeking international protection. Often conflicts about the human rights of migrants arise in respect to people who are seeking or have sought international protection. However, as noted earlier, the international framework of refugee rights is much better defined than that of migrants who are not refugees. It is therefore particularly important that the New York Declaration reaffirms States' commitment to the Universal Declaration of Human Rights (the Universal Declaration) and the core UN human rights treaties. Indeed, human rights are referred to more than 30 times in the New York Declaration and in the section specific to the Global Compact on Migration 11 times.[15] The Compact must implement the objectives of the General Assembly set out in the New York Declaration. Thus the Compact on Safe, Orderly and Regular Migration will need to build on the existing international human rights of migrants.

Secondly, this book is intended to assist officials, lawyers and academics to ensure that the human rights of migrants are fully respected by State authorities and international organisations and safeguarded by national and supranational courts across the globe. Everyone has an interest in ensuring that State commitments are fully and properly respected. States voluntarily enter into international agreements which create obligations for them. They do so in accordance with their constitutional arrangements which engage their State. Having done so, States are committed to ensuring that their national law and its application by their officials, agencies and the private sector fully complies with these obligations arising from international law. Their courts, other dispute resolution mechanisms and complaints bodies must be able to take their State's international obligations into account when examining the application of national laws to ensure compliance.

Human rights are not simply for citizens, they are for everyone. Migrants are just as entitled to respect and State compliance with (almost) all human rights as citizens of a State. This is the principle of equal treatment and non-discrimination, which is a human right in itself contained in all the nine core human rights conventions. There are two types of exceptions in international human rights law. The first type of exception is in respect of rights which on their face exclude migrants and which are mainly limited to the fields of democratic process (such as voting rights). We will not dwell on these exceptions, as they are explicit in human rights conventions and very few in number. The second type of exception is very different – these exceptions permit States to limit certain human rights (but not all) where this is justified on the grounds enumerated in the convention. While some human rights can be subject to limitations, such as the right to family life, others are absolute, such as the prohibition on torture or return to a country where there is a substantial risk that the person would suffer torture. It is always for the State to justify its use of an exception setting out the grounds on which it is relying and the circumstances which justify it. Where a State is entitled to limit a human right on a ground of an exception, it must start from the position that everyone is entitled to the right equally. The scope of the exception must not discriminate on the basis that the person claiming the right is a citizen or a migrant unless the State can justify the difference in treatment and show that it is proportionate to the objective sought.

Sometimes, States confuse the two types of exception. They may claim the right to treat migrants differently from their citizens on the basis of national security or public policy. This can only be justified in international human rights law. When States seek to rely on exceptions which are permitted by international human rights law in respect of some rights, the scope of those exceptions should be the same whether the person is a citizen or a migrant. This is because everyone is entitled to the human right to equal treatment and non-discrimination.

The rights explained in this book are all grounded in the Universal Declaration, which forms the modern basis of States' human rights duties. The rights are provided in a definitive legal form in the nine human rights conventions which constitute the UN's core human rights instruments.[16] These human rights conventions are subject to interpretation and clarification by the Treaty Bodies established according to the provisions of each convention for this purpose. These Treaty Bodies have both a definitive interpretative duty regarding the meaning of the conventions' provisions and a dispute resolution role regarding individual complaints against States regarding respect for the human rights set out in the conventions.[17] The Treaty Bodies hear complaints by individuals and determine the legality of State action. In this book, we examine the clarifications and determinations of the Treaty Bodies regarding the correct interpretation of States' human rights obligations towards migrants under the conventions. This book is not aspirational – it does not set out what we might consider, in our personal capacities, to be the best rights for migrants. We set out the existing state of the law as laid down in the conventions and interpreted by the Treaty Bodies. We have, however, on occasion, also included interpretative guidance from the Treaty Bodies (or UNHCR), which is less authoritative than the Opinions, Decisions and General Comments of the Treaty Bodies.

The Migrant Workers Convention has particular relevance to this book not least because the New York Declaration calls on all States to ratify it. But we have not placed it at the centre of our examination because many States which consider themselves to be destinations of migrants have not ratified it yet. The Migrant Workers Convention primarily consolidates rights for migrant workers which come from other human rights conventions. By creating a convention on the rights of migrant workers, some States have suggested that where States decline to ratify the convention, they can escape their pre-existing obligations to protect migrants' human rights. This is a fallacious argument. Just because the personal scope is limited in this one treaty to migrants, it cannot limit the scope of application of the same rights in other treaties which apply to everyone. The argument that this convention is *lex specialis* for migrants' rights cannot, as a consequence, diminish the human rights migrants are entitled to under other human rights conventions.[18]

We are very grateful to the work which others have undertaken and which is central to our examination here. In particular, we are most grateful to the OHCHR, which has issued a series of substantial reports and guidelines on the subject of human rights and migrants starting with Improving the Human Rights–Based Governance of International Migration.[19] The Human Rights Committee's insistence on the need for a holistic approach to the protection of migrants' human rights is key. The field is often fragmented according to the category of migrant – i.e., refugee, trafficked person, child. This fragmentation has been unhelpful to the recognition of the framework of human rights applicable to all migrants. We are also grateful to the excellent work done by colleagues at Georgetown University setting out the International Migrants Bill of Rights, which provides an excellent review of all human rights as they apply to migrants.[20] We strongly recommend this work, which is both accessible and comprehensive. There are also other initiatives which are authoritative and valuable, and it is within the range of available work on the subject that we publish this book to assist in the formation of the Global Compact on Migration.

The human rights of migrants

All human rights are important for migrants, but some provide solutions to problems which they encounter because they are not citizens of the State where they live. The reason is very simple. The claim of States to control the movement of persons across State borders divides the citizens from migrants. People are categorised as citizens or migrants at State borders[21] by virtue of the State's claim to sovereignty at the border. This is a moment of great vulnerability for the individual. While the citizen is protected by the State's constitution on entering his or her State, the migrant is no longer protected by his or her State's constitution by virtue of the act of crossing the border out of the territory. Whether the migrant at the border will be admitted or not is a cherished State sovereign claim which has become an increasing strident in the twenty-first century.[22] National laws which determine the powers of State authorities regarding admission of migrants tend to leave wide discretion to officials. The legal vulnerability of the migrant at the border of a State seeking admission then follows him or her within the State through the differentiation of rights and entitlements on the basis of citizenship. Citizens have a right to enter, reside and work in their State both under national and international law simply because they are recognised by their State as citizens. They are also protected against removal.[23] But the migrant does not necessarily enjoy these rights automatically. The difference of treatment between the citizen and the migrant is a contested field of discrimination where the migrants' vulnerability to refusal of admission and removal are key to justifications of discrimination. Where particular tensions arise between migrants and States, the correct application of international human rights law regarding this difference in treatment is important. The question which so often arises is whether the treatment is prohibited discrimination or different treatment justified because the two categories (citizen and migrant) are not comparable (we will return to this issue later).

The vulnerability of the migrant to be refused admission to a State and/ or removal from the State can be a very strong obstacle to the enjoyment of other human rights. People may be dissuaded from seeking to enjoy their human rights if, by claiming those rights, they risk exclusion or removal from the State. 'Making do' with substandard treatment by State and private actors (treatment which is not consistent with the State's obligations under human rights conventions to which it is a party) is the outcome of this vulnerability. How does human rights law help both State authorities and migrants clarify the scope of this vulnerability and resolve tensions regarding the rights of migrants? We start from the documents in which the obligations are found.

Dignity, discrimination or differential treatment

The Universal Declaration is the starting point of UN post-WWII human rights. It commences with the acknowledgement that 'whereas recognition of the inherent dignity and of the equal and inalienable rights of all members of the human family is the foundation of freedom, justice and peace in the world'. Human dignity is the starting place of all human rights and the foundation of them. The central framing of 'inherent dignity' in the Universal Declaration reflects an understanding of the goal of human rights – to ensure that each individual can lead a life of dignity. It is through human rights – both the extension of them and, most importantly, substantive access to them in practice – that individuals can lead dignified lives. Equality and the right to non-discrimination are key ways to realise dignity. This is just as true for migrants as for citizens.

The Human Rights Committee in General Comment No. 15 issued in 1986 on 'the position of aliens under the Covenant' held the following:

1   In general, the rights set forth in the Covenant apply to everyone, irrespective of reciprocity, and irrespective of his or her nationality or statelessness.

2   Thus, the general rule is that each one of the rights of the Covenant must be guaranteed without discrimination between citizens and aliens. Aliens receive the benefit of the general requirement of non-discrimination in respect of the rights guaranteed in the Covenant, as provided for in article 2 thereof. This guarantee applies to aliens and citizens alike. Exceptionally, some of the rights recognized in the Covenant are expressly applicable only to citizens (art. 25), while article 13 applies only to aliens.

Article 2 Civil Rights Covenant sets out the prohibition on discrimination.[24] The wording of the provision does not explicitly prohibit discrimination on the basis of nationality. But it does prohibit discrimination on the basis of national origin. States have long (and successfully) claimed that discrimination on the basis of national origin is different from discrimination on the basis of nationality. However, discrimination on one of the prohibited grounds (such as religion, political opinion, national origin or race) may be hidden behind discrimination on the basis of nationality. There can be a human rights problem with the duty of non-discrimination when prohibited grounds of discrimination lurk behind a State's claim to the legitimacy of differential treatment between citizens and migrants or between migrants only on the basis of their nationality. Similarly, the list of prohibited grounds of discrimination is not closed – it includes 'other status'. This must include migratory status which results in the denial of equality in respect to human rights.

Discrimination and access to territory

Article 13 of the Universal Declaration[25] clarifies the right of all people whether within or outside their countries to enter 'their' country and to leave, as well as the right to move within the State. The right to move across borders, albeit always stressed by those favouring hard border controls on migrants, is not accompanied by an explicit right to enter any other country. The intersection of the right to leave and return to one's country with the right to non-discrimination in the enjoyment of rights in the Universal Declaration constitutes an important foundation of the rights of migrants. Article 13 of the Universal Declaration is given more definition in Article 12 of the Civil Rights Covenant.[26] Again, the right is that to leave a country, notably not accompanied by a right to enter another. Yet this is neither the end of the matter nor a triumph of State sovereign claims regarding border controls.

The Human Rights Committee in its General Comment 27 (1999) clarified that the scope of application of Article 12.[27] Paragraph 20 of the General Comment is particularly important for the Global Compact:

> 20 [The Covenant][28] does not distinguish between nationals and aliens ('no one'). Thus, the persons entitled to exercise this right can be identified only by interpreting the meaning of the phrase 'his own country'[29] . . . The scope of 'his own country' is broader than the concept 'country of his nationality'. It is not limited to nationality in a formal sense, that is, nationality acquired at birth or by conferral; it embraces, at the very least, an individual who, because of his or her special ties to or claims in relation to a given country, cannot be considered to be a mere alien. This would be the case, for example, of nationals of a country who have there been stripped of their nationality in violation of international law, and of individuals whose country of nationality has been incorporated in or transferred to another national entity, whose nationality is being denied them. The [Covenant], moreover, permits a broader interpretation that might embrace other categories of long-term residents, including but not limited to stateless persons arbitrarily deprived of the right to acquire the nationality of the country of such residence.[30]

This clarification provides States with an excellent starting place to understand the nexus between their duty not to discrimination and the difference between citizens and migrants. We will return evaluating this issue of the right to leave and the ambiguity of entry in Chapter 6.

Discrimination and rights

At the centre of the issues which migrants face in seeking to enjoy their human rights is the differential treatment between citizens and migrants which State authorities claim is a legitimate exercise of State sovereignty. This argument is frequently premised on the claim that citizens and migrants are so profoundly different that treating them differently is not discrimination at all. It is simply differential treatment outside the scope of any non-discrimination obligation. This argument is incorrect and a legally unsustainable interpretation of Article 2 of the Civil Rights Covenant.

The Human Rights Committee dealt with this central issue of discrimination versus differential treatment between citizens and migrants in 2004 when it published General Comment No. 31 including an important clarification of the scope of Article 2 of the Civil Rights Covenant:

> 10 [States] are required to respect and to ensure the Covenant rights to all persons who may be within their territory and to all persons subject to their jurisdiction. This means that a State party must respect and ensure the rights laid down in the Covenant to anyone within the power or effective control of that State Party, even if not situated within the territory of the State Party. As indicated in General Comment 15 adopted at the twenty-seventh session (1986), the enjoyment of Covenant rights is not limited to citizens of States Parties but must also be available to all individuals, regardless of nationality or statelessness, such as asylum seekers, refugees, migrant workers and other persons, who may find themselves in the territory or subject to the jurisdiction of the State Party. This principle also applies to those within the power or effective control of the forces of a State Party acting outside its territory, regardless of the circumstances in which such power or effective control was obtained, such as forces constituting a national contingent of a State Party assigned to an international peace-keeping or peace-enforcement operation.

On this legal point, we are ready to examine the issues and problems of migrants from the perspective of the human rights obligations of States, which can assist to resolve them. We recommend that the reader always bear in mind the question, is this human right different for a citizen and a migrant, and if so, on what grounds can it be different? Differential treatment between the two groups of people, unless sufficiently justified, is discrimination. Discrimination is contrary to the principle of human dignity, which must inform all human rights, as it is their objective.

The human rights applicable to the problems of migrants will be dealt with in the following chapters:

2) The right to be recognised as a person before the law: what does it mean to have a human right to be recognised as a person? How

does international law describe this right and its consequences for the migrant? This chapter examines the entitlement to personhood, which is essential to the establishment of other human rights claims.

3) Migrants' rights at the border: States have a sovereign right to control who enters their territory but what does this mean for migrants standing at the border, and how they are treated? What are their human rights when they are seeking entry to a State? This chapter examines the duties of States towards migrants at the border.

4) Immigration detention: where States refuse migrants entry to the territory or seek to expel them, immigration detention is a common intermediate outcome for the individual. What are the limitations on immigration detention which international human rights obligations place on States? In this chapter, the limitations on detention of people simply because they are migrants are set out.

5) Irregular status: States frequently categorise migrants as regular or irregular depending on whether the authorities have chosen to issue a person with a residence document or not. What are the human rights of those to whom the State has not issued or has refused documents? This chapter looks at the international standards relevant to this issue.

6) Rights of residence, termination of residence and in respect to removal: what human rights do migrants have when they claim residence and protection against removal? What are the sources of these rights, and how do they arise? This chapter examines the human rights issues which arise in respect to migrants' claims to residence.

7) The economic, social and cultural rights of migrants: migrants become part of the States where they live, and they exercise economic, social and cultural rights there. What is the human rights basis of these rights? What are migrants entitled to as regards inclusion in society? International human rights law includes extensive State obligations regarding economic social and cultural rights. These are examined in this chapter.

8) Rights at work: migrants usually want to work in their host State; what rights do they have to do so and what conditions can States place on migrants' working conditions and pay? International labour standards are key to this chapter.

9) Family life and the migrant: after entry, residence and work, migrants seek to enjoy family life in their host State. This will include family reunification with members of their families who are also migrants. What are these rights in international human

rights law? This chapter details the sources of these rights and the limitations which States can legitimately place on them.

10) Freedom of thought, belief and religion and freedom of expression and opinion: migrants are entitled to freedom of thought, belief, religion and expression in human rights law; what does this mean as regards the exercise of these rights? These are real rights for migrants as well as citizens. This chapter sets out their scope and what limitations are permissible.

11) The right to an effective remedy, the right to an effective national procedure against arbitrary removal and the right to a fair hearing: rights without remedies are never real for those who want to use them. So procedural rights are a necessary component to the human rights of migrants. What is this right to an effective remedy, and what does it encompass?

These are the central issues which we will develop in the following chapters. As we follow the migrant's trajectory through time, space and sovereign State claims, we will examine the human rights obligations which may help the migrant to achieve his or her objectives and the duties of States to achieve their human rights commitments including towards migrants. Human rights are the creation of States. States voluntarily enter into their human rights commitments. Human rights must never be construed by States as obstacles to political objectives. Political objectives must be crafted to respect and further State's human rights obligations.

Notes

1 A/71/L.1 para 5.
2 The New York Declaration.
3 This is a term 'Global Compact' which has only rarely been used by the UN the legal impact of which remains fluid.
4 A/71/L.1 para 22.
5 A/71/L.1 para 41.
6 A/71/L.1 para 64.
7 Guild, E., S. Grant, and K. Groenendijk. "IOM and the UN: Unfinished Business." (2017) papers.ssrn.com.
8 There is one exception – in the chapter on irregular status, we have used a decision of a regional court.
9 In this book, we focus primarily on international human rights as contained in the UN conventions, but we also include international labour rights contained in the ILO's conventions where relevant to migrants. This is particularly the case in Chapter 8.
10 In this document, we use the term migrant to mean anyone who is not a citizen of the State where he or she is present. The most common term used before the mid-1980s was 'alien', still a stalwart of international law; subsequently,

'foreigner' was often deployed. The UN General Assembly's resolution calling for the establishment of a Global Compact for Safe, Orderly and Regulation Migration uses the term migrant. As this work is designed to provide guidance to the process of the Global Compact (in addition to other purposes), we use the term migrant.

11 Human Rights Committee General Comment 31 CCPR/C/21/Rev.1/Add. 1326 May 2004.

12 Human Rights Committee in General Comment No. 15 on "the position of aliens under the Covenant" issued in 1986.

13 Civil and Political Rights Covenant Article 2:
   3 Each State Party to the present Covenant undertakes:

   (a)   To ensure that any person whose rights or freedoms as herein recognized are violated shall have an effective remedy, notwithstanding that the violation has been committed by persons acting in an official capacity;

   (b)   To ensure that any person claiming such a remedy shall have his right thereto determined by competent judicial, administrative or legislative authorities, or by any other competent authority provided for by the legal system of the State, and to develop the possibilities of judicial remedy;

   (c)   To ensure that the competent authorities shall enforce such remedies when granted.

14 www.un.org/ga/search/view_doc.asp?symbol=A/71/L.1 [accessed 15 February 2017].

15 Paragraphs 5, 6, 11, 22, 24, 26, 32, 41, 47, 51, 59.

16 www.ohchr.org/EN/ProfessionalInterest/Pages/CoreInstruments.aspx [accessed 15 February 2017]. Some rights permit derogation in exceptional circumstances. The purpose of this paper is not to examine those exceptions which have been well discussed elsewhere. See, for instance, Rainey, B., E. Wicks, and C. Ovey, *Jacobs, White and Ovey: The European Convention on Human Rights.* Oxford: Oxford University Press, 2014.

17 States are entitled to accept or refuse the jurisdiction of the Treaty Bodies to adjudicate individual complaints against them.

18 The lack of extensive ratification of this convention by major receiving countries in North America and Europe (with the notable exceptions of Mexico and Turkey) is often used to undermine the applicability of all human rights conventions to migrants. This is a specious argument which is legally incorrect.

19 Available at www.ohchr.org/EN/Issues/TransnationalCorporations/Pages/Reports.aspx [accessed 26 April 2017].

20 www.law.georgetown.edu/academics/centers-institutes/isim/imbr/ [accessed 15 February 2017].

21 For visa nationals, this process starts even within the territory of their own State.

22 Biersteker, T. J., "State, Sovereignty and Territory," *Handbook of International Relations* (2002): 157–176.

23 Throughout this book, we use the term 'removal', which is wider than expulsion and generically clearer than deportation. Where a provision of law or reference to a Treaty Body finding or comment is quoted, we retain the original wording.

24 Civil and Political Rights Covenant Article 2.

   1   Each State Party to the present Covenant undertakes to respect and to ensure to all individuals within its territory and subject to its jurisdiction

the rights recognized in the present Covenant, without distinction of any kind, such as race, colour, sex, language, religion, political or other opinion, national or social origin, property, birth or other status.

2   Where not already provided for by existing legislative or other measures, each State Party to the present Covenant undertakes to take the necessary steps, in accordance with its constitutional processes and with the provisions of the present Covenant, to adopt such laws or other measures as may be necessary to give effect to the rights recognized in the present Covenant.

25 (1) Everyone has the right to freedom of movement and residence within the borders of each state.

     (2) Everyone has the right to leave any country, including his own, and to return to his country.

26 Article 12

1   Everyone lawfully within the territory of a State shall, within that territory, have the right to liberty of movement and freedom to choose his residence.

2   Everyone shall be free to leave any country, including his own.

3   The above-mentioned rights shall not be subject to any restrictions except those which are provided by law, are necessary to protect national security, public order (ordre public), public health or morals or the rights and freedoms of others, and are consistent with the other rights recognized in the present Covenant.

4   No one shall be arbitrarily deprived of the right to enter his own country.

27 Human Rights Committee General Comment No. 27: Article 12 (Freedom of Movement), 2 November 1999, CCPR/C/21/Rev.1/Add.9, available at www.refworld.org/docid/45139c394.html [accessed 15 January 2017].

28 Article 12(4).

29 See communication No. 538/1993, Stewart v. Canada.

30 Article 12(4).

2   The right to be recognised as a person before the law[1]

Kathryn Allinson

Recognition as a person before the law protects an individual's ability to 'vote, marry or secure formal employment . . . obtain a driver's license, to open a bank account, to have access to social security or a pension, to obtain insurance or a line of credit, and, significantly, to be able to register one's own children.' Denial of the right can lead to enforced or involuntary disappearances, statelessness, early and forced marriage, trafficking, child labour and the sale of children. It also affects access to the right to education and right to health.

Source: OHCHR, Birth registration and the right of everyone to recognition everywhere as a person before the law (2014) A/HRC/27/22 para 17, 18–32.

> Everyone has the right to recognition as a person before the law.
> New York Declaration of the UN General
> Assembly 19 September 2016[2]

Prohibiting 'civil death'

Deprivation of an individual's capacity to be a person before the law has been described as 'civil death' because it degrades him or her to become an 'outlawed' legal object in contravention of Article 16 of the Civil and Political Rights Covenant.[3] For example, under Roman law and in more recent legal systems slaves were stripped of all legal rights and reduced to legal objects upon which the owner had the power of life and death.[4] It is essential to protect migrants from being robbed of their personality before the law, making them dependent on the mercy or arbitrariness of society. Denial of legal personality, even as a punishment, is a breach of human rights law. The right applies equally to all people within a State's jurisdiction, including migrants held in detention centers or those who have irregularly entered the country. States must not deny the legal personhood of any migrant, irregular or otherwise.

The right to recognition as person before the law is a non-derogable right enshrined in the Universal Declaration and the Civil and Political Rights Covenant:

> Everyone shall have the right to recognition everywhere as a person before the law.[5]

Recognition as a person before the law includes legal personality, juridical personality, capacity to have rights, legal capacity, capacity to act, competence, and autonomy.[6] This right recognises the existence of the individual as a human being with distinct needs, interests, and opinions, and is 'a necessary prerequisite to all other rights of the individual.'[7] Nowak notes,

> Without this right, the individual could be degraded to a mere legal object, where he or she would no longer be a person in the legal sense and thus be deprived of all other rights, including the right to life.[8]

This is the essence of the right to recognition as a person before the law in the Civil and Political Rights Covenant.[9] A legal person 'enjoys, and is subject to, rights and duties at law'.[10] It is central to the conception of human rights, as it expresses the right and the capacity of each human being to be the holder of rights and obligations under the law.[11] The 'capacity to be a person before the law' endows the individual with the right to have his or her status and capacity recognised in the legal order. Legal personality is a crucial aspect of freedom, as

> [i]t distinguishes one man from others and permits him to assert his essential dignity *erga omnes*. It concentrates the attention of the legal order upon each human being. It gives to the essential dignity of the human being reality in law. Without it, man would not be truly free, for he would be subject to injustice and injury without legal remedy.[12]

Scope of the right

Logically, the capacity for legal personhood starts with birth and ends with death.[13] An analysis of the Civil and Political Rights Covenant makes clear that Article 16 only covers the capacity to be a person before the law, not the capacity to act.[14] The inclusion of 'recognition' in Article 16 implies a State must actively recognise the right in its law, not merely concede to it.[15] The inclusion of 'everywhere' asserts that individuals must be found to have legal personhood wherever they are by the State in whose territory they find themselves.[16] The Human Rights Committee has affirmed that

States cannot deny an individual their legal personhood, even by removing them from territory or jurisdiction: 'Intentionally removing a person from the protection of the law for a prolonged period of time may constitute a refusal of recognition as a person before the law'.[17]

In General Comment 28 (on the equality of rights between men and women), the Human Rights Committee explained that denying women the ability to enter into contracts or to own property, because they are women, prevents them 'from functioning as full legal persons' for discriminatory reasons and is in breach of Article 16'.[18] The implication is that, failing to provide complete legal recognition and exposing a group of human beings to legal incapacity without reasonable justification can amount to a breach of Article 16. As such, States cannot deny any group, including migrants, irrespective of their immigration status, their rights to legal personhood whether by limiting their legal personality or by removal from a territory.

Rights of migrants to be recognised as a person before the law

According to Article 16 of the Civil and Political Rights Covenant, 'every-one' – women and men, children of both sexes, citizens, foreigners and stateless persons – have the right to have their status and capacity recognised in the legal order.[19] In addition, in the Migrant Workers Convention, Article 24 says, 'Every migrant worker and every member of his or her family shall have the right to recognition everywhere as a person before the law'.[20] As such, all migrants, irrespective of their immigration status, must be treated as people before the law, worthy of rights, autonomy, and legal capacity.

How do migrants prove they are a human with human rights?

If it is impossible for citizens from other countries to prove their identity and family relations through national documents, the result is that these persons do not 'exist' before the law.[21] As a result, there is an obligation on a receiving State to facilitate migrants in becoming administratively 'visible'.[22] Boeles explains that States can guarantee this by recognising documents from the migrant's homeland, even if the administration in that country is far from reliable, or by providing replacement documents which enable the migrant to prove who he or she is and legally to participate in the host society.[23] It is essential that migrants be protected by the provisions of the law in order to avoid the breach of their right to legal personhood.

The right to have one's birth registered, as secured in the Convention of the Rights of the Child, is a fundamental element of the right to be recognised as a person before the law.[24] Birth registration is integral for being recognised as a person before the law; it provides an individual the material evidence to prove his or her legal personality. The UNHCR has consistently raised the issue of birth registration of refugees, asylum seekers and stateless persons in its 'Conclusions on International Protection' as essential for avoiding human rights abuses.[25] In addition, the rights of migrants to have civil documents ensures that migrants have the procedural aspects of legal personhood.[26] A substantial part of the cases of statelessness is caused by lack of birth certificates and comparable documents.[27] As a result, the right to be recognised as a person before the law must be protected for migrants by the material access to identity documents and by having those documents recognised by the State.

Conclusion

The right to be recognised before the law is essential for ensuring the protection of an individual's human rights and autonomy. States must

1   Ensure migrants, irrespective of their immigration status, are considered a person before the law and the rights related to this: fair trial, remedies, equality before the law, non-discrimination; and
2   Recognise, or replace, civil documents of migrants, who are involuntarily without them, in order to avoid their 'civil death'.

Notes

1   Due to lack of guidelines on Article 16, this chapter includes opinio juris and scholarly articles to inform the scope of the human right.
2   A/71/L.1 para 13.
3   Such actions 'would in and of itself hardly represent a violation of any provision other than Article 16'. In Nowak, M., *U.N. Covenant on Civil and Political Rights: CCPR Commentary*. Germany: N.P. Engel Publisher, 2005, p. 373.
4   For examples of deprivation of legal personality in modern times, see Nowak, M., *U.N. Covenant on Civil and Political Rights: CCPR Commentary*. N.P. Engel Publisher, 2005, and Joseph, S., J. Schultz, and M. Castan, *The International Covenant on Civil and Political Rights: Cases, Materials, and Commentary*, 2nd edition. Oxford: Oxford University Press, 2004, p. 299.
5   The text in both authorities is identical. See Universal Declaration Article 6, Civil and Political Rights Covenant Article 16.
6   Brett, M., "The Right to Recognition as a Person before the Law and the Capacity to Act under International Human Rights Law," *Irish Centre for Human Rights* (2012): 9.

7   Van Bueren, G., *The International Law on the Rights of the Child*. Boston: Martinus Nijhoff, 1995, p. 40.
8   Nowak, M., *U.N. Covenant on Civil and Political Rights: CCPR Commentary*. N.P. Engel Publisher, 2005, p. 369.
9   Ibid.
10 Osborn, P. G. *A Concise Law Dictionary-For Students and Practitioners*. Read Books Ltd, 2013.
11 Working Group on Enforced or Involuntary Disappearances, General Comment on the right to recognition as a person before the law in the context of enforced disappearances (2012 A/HRC/19/58/Rev.1) para 4.
12 Volio, F., Legal Personality, Privacy, and the Family, in Henkin, L. (Ed.), *The International Bill of Rights: The Covenant on Civil and Political Rights*. New York: Columbia University Press, 1981, p. 186.
13 Nowak, M., *U.N. Covenant on Civil and Political Rights: CCPR Commentary*. N.P. Engel Publisher, 2005, 369.
14 Bossuyt, M.J., *Guide to the "Travaux Préparatoires" of the International Covenant on Civil and Political Rights*. Boston: Martinus Nijhoff, 1987, p. 335.
15 OHCHR, Background conference document prepared by the Office of the United Nations High Commissioner for Human Rights: Legal Capacity (2005) para 7.
16 Ibid.
17 Human Rights Committee, Communication No. 2051/2011 (UN. Doc. CCPR/C/112/D/2051/2011). See also Report of the Working Group Enforced or Involuntary Disappearances, E/CN.4/1435, § 184).
18 OHCHR, General Comment No 28: Article 3, The equality of rights between men and women (CCPR/C/21/Rev.1/Add.10, 29 March 2000) para 19
19 OHCHR para 7.
20 Migrant Workers Convention Article 24.
21 See Avellanal v. Peru (202/86), De Gallicio and Vicario v. Argentine (400/90), Inostraza a.o. v. Cile (717/96, and Varga v. Chile (717/96).
22 Boeles, P.B., *Mensen & Papieren: legalisatie en verificatie van bultenlandse documenten in 'probleemlanden'*. Utrecht: FORUM, 2003.
23 Ibid.
24 Child Rights Convention Article 7; Civil and Political Rights Covenant Article 24(2); Migrant Workers Convention, Article 29; Convention on the Rights of Persons with Disabilities Article 18.
25 Executive Committee UNHCR, Conclusion on International Protection (No. 111 (LXIV)-2013, October 2013) See also Framework for the Protection of Children, available at: www.refworld.org/docid/4fe875682.html.
26 Refugee Convention Article 12, 15, 27; UN General Assembly, Convention Relating to the Status of Stateless Persons (28 September 1954, United Nations) Article 28.
27 Van Waas, L., *Nationality Matters: Statelessness Under International Law*. Intersentia, 2008, pp. 95, 163.

3   Migrants' rights at the border

Ceren Mutus Toprakseven

A migrant (also a dual national of the state) was stopped at the airport on her departure and taken into custody without explanation by the authorities of the state and held without knowledge of where she was being held or why for more than a month.

Opinion No. 28/2016 concerning Nazanin Zaghari-Ratcliffe (Islamic Republic of Iran) violation of Civil and Political Rights Covenant, Working Group on Arbitrary Detention at its seventy-sixth session, 22–26 August 2016.

> We are committed to protecting the safety, dignity and human rights and fundamental freedoms of all migrants, regardless of their migratory status at all times.
>
> New York Declaration of the UN General Assembly
> 19 September 2016[1]

Principle of non-discrimination

While States have the sovereign right to control their borders and regulate the conditions of entry and stay of migrants in their territory, this right is not absolute and, instead, is subject to legal limitations set by international human rights law.[2] In this regard, one of the fundamental principles recognised by international and regional human rights instruments is that of non-discrimination, which implies that everyone is entitled to human rights protection, regardless of their legal status, nationality or other grounds. Differential treatment between citizens and migrants may be permitted only under limited circumstances and these exceptions should be interpreted narrowly.

International human rights law provides clear constraints on States' immigration and border policies, including entry decisions. The UN Human Rights Committee, in its General Comment No. 15, submits that under certain circumstances, migrants may enjoy the protection of the Civil and Political Rights Covenant, 'even in relation to entry or residence, for example, when considerations of non-discrimination, prohibition of inhuman treatment and respect for family life arise'.[3] Similarly, the Covenant prohibits discrimination 'in law or in fact in any field regulated and protected by public authorities'.[4]

Thus, when conducting border measures, States should abstain from discriminating against migrants on the basis of, inter alia, national or social origin, religion, race, colour, age, sexual orientation or gender identity, political opinion, migration status and economic and social situation.[5] Nationality is a prohibited ground of discrimination. Article 1(3) ICERD stipulates that 'Nothing in this Convention may be interpreted as affecting in any way the legal provisions of States Parties concerning nationality, citizenship or naturalization, provided that such provisions do not discriminate against any particular nationality'.[6] Similarly, the General Recommendation No. 30 adopted by the Committee on the Elimination of Racial Discrimination (the Treaty Body of ICERD) states that States 'ensure that immigration policies do not have the effect of discriminating against persons on the basis of race, colour, descent, or national or ethnic origin'.[7]

Where differential treatment is contemplated, it must pursue a legitimate aim and be proportional to the achievement of this objective.[8] Particularly, border measures employed to address irregular migration, transnational organised crime or international terrorism shall not be discriminatory 'in purpose or effect'.[9]

Respect for human dignity

States should design and implement their immigration and border policies with full respect for the inherent dignity of migrants. The Universal Declaration affirms this principle: 'All human beings are born free and equal in dignity'.[10]

The 2001 Recommendation issued by the Council of Europe Commissioner for Human Rights includes, inter alia, the following paragraph on human dignity:

> Everyone has the right, on arrival at the border of a Member State, to be treated with respect for his or her *human dignity* rather than automatically considered to be a criminal or guilty of fraud.[11]

Closely linked with the principle of respect for human dignity, migrants at international borders should be protected against arbitrary arrest or detention.[12] States should consider detention as a last resort and ensure that 'the reasons for any detention are clearly defined in law, of limited scope and duration, necessary and proportionate, and that reasons for such detention are explained to migrants'.[13] To comply with the principles of legality and proportionality, States should introduce procedural safeguards including 'judicial authorisation and oversight, possibility to appeal and legal aid'[14] (see Chapters 4 and 11). In this vein, the Working Group on Arbitrary Detention has submitted that arbitrary detention can occur 'when asylum seekers, immigrants or refugees are subjected to prolonged administrative custody without possibility of administrative or judicial review or remedy'.[15]

Where less intrusive measures are found inadequate and detention is used, migrants should still be treated in accordance with international human rights standards. They should have unconditional access to medical and health care, and such care should be delivered by qualified personnel who take into consideration the specific needs of the detained migrant.[16] Similarly, interviews should be conducted by border officials

> in a professional, open and non-threatening way, in a private and appropriate place with adequate facilities to meet basic needs, and with the clear objective of appropriately referring migrants who may be at particular risk at international borders to competent authorities.[17]

Last but not least, migrants in detention should be provided unconditional access to 'competent, free and independent legal aid' to exercise their right to judicial review of their detention.[18]

Principle of *non-refoulement*

The principle of *non-refoulement*, which constitutes one of the fundamental safeguards pertaining to the entry and stay of a migrant in a foreign territory, is aimed at precluding States from returning any person, regardless of nationality, status or other grounds, to places where they might be exposed to torture, inhuman and degrading treatment or punishment.[19] Well established in international human rights and refugee law instruments, the principle is widely considered as international customary law and therefore binding on all States.[20]

The principle is explicit in Article 3 Convention against Torture, which bars the State Party from 'expel[ing], return[ing] ("*refouler*") or extradit[ing] a person to another State where there are substantial grounds for believing that he would be in danger of being subjected to torture'. The Committee against Torture stressed that States should also refrain from transferring an individual to any country other than his own, where he faces the risk of subsequent refoulement.[21]

Although the Civil and Political Rights Covenant does not expressly refer to the principle of *non-refoulement*, the Human Rights Committee has interpreted Article 7 to encompass returns to places where the individuals might be exposed to the

> real risk of irreparable harm such as that contemplated by Articles 6 and 7 of the Covenant, either in the country to which removal is to be effected or in any country to which the person may subsequently be removed.[22]

As in the context of the Convention against Torture, *non-refoulement* protections are applied to everyone, and no derogation is permitted.

Protection against collective removal

Protection from collective removal is a fundamental human right granted to migrants at the border. It is understood as 'any measure compelling aliens, as a group, to leave a country, except where such a measure is taken on the basis of a reasonable and objective examination of the particular case of each individual alien of the group'.[23] While not preventing the State from expelling several people simultaneously, the prohibition of collective removal requires that 'each person concerned is given the opportunity to put arguments against his/her expulsion to the competent authorities on an individual basis'.[24]

The prohibition is well established in international human rights law. The Civil and Political Rights Covenant has confirmed that 'laws or decisions providing for collective or mass expulsions' would constitute a violation of Article 13 Civil and Political Rights Covenant.[25] Likewise, Article 22(1) of the Migrant Workers Convention provides that 'migrant workers and members of their families shall not be subject to measures of collective removal. Each case of removal shall be examined and decided individually'.

Conclusion

In conclusion, when conducting border control measures, States should comply with the following international principles:

1   Migrants at international borders should not be subject to discrimination based on any prohibited grounds.
2   Migrants should be treated with respect for their human dignity. In this respect, they should be protected against arbitrary arrest or detention. If detention is necessary, States should ensure that migrants are provided unconditional access to legal aid. Moreover, migrants held in detention should benefit from professional medical and health care, if needed.

3   States should respect the fundamental principle of *non-refoulement* and refrain from sending anyone, including migrants, to places where they might be exposed to torture, inhuman and degrading treatment or punishment. This prohibition also applies to cases where the individual faces the risk of indirect refoulement.

4   Similarly, States should not engage in practices of collective removal. Any decision of removal should be examined and decided individually.

Notes

1   A/71/L.1 para 41.
2   Taylor-Nicholson, E. and P. Oberoi, "Background Paper: OHCHR in Cooperation with the GAATW Expert Consultation on Human Rights at International Borders: Exploring Gaps in Policy and Practice", (March 2012) pp. 5–6.
3   UN Human Rights Committee, General Comment No. 15: The Position of Aliens Under the Covenant, 11 April 1986, para 5.
4   Human Rights Committee, General Comment No. 18: Non-discrimination, 10 November 1989, para 12.
5   OHCHR Recommended Principles and Guidelines on Human Rights at International Borders, A/69/CRP.1, 24 October 2014, p. 8.
6   ICERD, art. 1(3); Migrant Workers Convention, art. 7.
7   CERD Committee, 1 October 2002, para 9.
8   CERD Committee, General Recommendation XXX on Discrimination against Non-Citizens, 1 October 2002, para 4.
9   OHCHR Recommended Principles and Guidelines on Human Rights at International Borders, A/69/CRP.1, 24 October 2014, p. 8.
10   UDHR, art. 1.
11   The Council of Europe Commissioner of Human Rights, Recommendation concerning the rights of aliens wishing to enter a Council of Europe Member State and the enforcement of expulsion decisions", 19 September 2001, p. 3, para 1.
12   Universal Declaration Articles 3 and 9, Civil and Political Rights Covenant Article 9, Migrant Workers Convention Article 16(4) all prohibit individual or collective arbitrary arrest or detention.
13   OHCHR Recommended Principles and Guidelines on Human Rights at International Borders, A/69/CRP.1, 24 October 2014, p. 33.
14   Ibid.
15   Working Group on Arbitrary Detention, Report of the Working Group on Arbitration, A/HRC/22/44, para 38(d).
16   OHCHR Recommended Principles and Guidelines on Human Rights at International Borders, A/69/CRP.1, 24 October 2014, p. 35.
17   Ibid. p. 28.
18   Ibid. p. 35.
19   Lauterpacht, E. and D. Bethlehem, The Scope and Content of the Principle of Non-Refoulement: Opinion, in Feller, E., Turk, V. and Nicholson, F. (Eds.), *Refugee Protection in International Law: UNHCR's Global Consultations on International Protection*. Cambridge: Cambridge University Press, 2003, pp. 89–90.
20   Inter-American Court of Human Rights, Advisory Opinion on Juridical Condition and Rights of the Undocumented Migrant, OC-18/03, 17 September 2003, Concurring Opinion of Judge A. A. Cançado Trindade, para 217ff; Hong Kong,

Court of Final Appeal of the Hong Kong Special Administrative Region, C, KMF and BF v. Director of Immigration, Secretary for Security, Nos. 18, 19 and 20 of 2011 (31 January 2013) Intervention of the UNHCR.
21 Committee against Torture Communication No. 13/1993 Balabou Mutombo v. Switzerland (27 April 1994), para 9.1.
22 Human Rights Committee, General Comment No. 31[80]: The Nature of the General Legal Obligation Imposed on States Parties to the Covenant, 29 March 2004, CCPR/C/21/Rev.1/Add. 13, para 12.
23 Andric v. Sweden, Application No. 45917/99, Council of Europe: European Court of Human Rights, 23 February 1999, para 1; Conka v. Belgium, Application No. 51564/99, Council of Europe: European Court of Human Rights, 5 February 2002, para 59. The Inter-American Commission has also held that 'an expulsion becomes collective when the decision to expel is not based on individual cases but on group considerations, even if the group in question is not large'. IACHR, Report on Terrorism and Human Rights, OEA/Ser.L/V/II.116, Doc. 5, rev. 1 corr., 22 October 2002.
24 Andric v. Sweden, Application No. 45917/99, Council of Europe: European Court of Human Rights, 23 February 1999, para 1.
25 UN Human Rights Committee, General Comment No. 15: The Position of Aliens Under the Covenant, 11 April 1986.

4   Immigration detention

*Kathryn Allinson, Justine Stefanelli
and Katharine T. Weatherhead*

*A man was detained for over two years despite expert evidence that his pro-
longed detention was causing significant deterioration of his mental state.
He claimed that his detention was arbitrary.*

*C v Australia, Communication No. 900/1999, Human Rights Commit-
tee violation of the Civil and Political Rights Covenant UN Doc CCPR/
C/76/D/900/1999 (2002).*

> Reaffirming that all individuals who have crossed or are seeking to cross
> international borders are entitled to due process in the assessment of their
> legal status, entry and stay, we will consider reviewing policies that crimi-
> nalize cross-border movements. We will also pursue alternatives to deten-
> tion while these assessments are underway.
>   New York Declaration of the UN General Assembly
>   19 September 2016[1]

Immigration detention, for the purpose of this chapter, is any detention of
migrants for migration policy reasons, regardless of their status.[2] It does not
include detention following conviction of an offence as determined by a
court. Detention, or total confinement, 'is at the extreme end of a spectrum
of deprivations of liberty'.[3] Detention of migrants is not prohibited per se;[4]
however, States must comply with their obligations under human rights law.
In particular, the human rights to liberty and security are enshrined in international law and use of detention must be weighed against these rights.[5]
Other relevant rights include the right to dignity when imprisoned,[6] access
to justice,[7] and freedom from torture and degrading treatment.[8] The principle of non-discrimination between citizens and non-citizens is important
in this context and must be respected. The principle of non-discrimination
is the legal entitlement to enjoy one's human rights on an equal basis and
free from discrimination on grounds of race, colour, sex, sexual orientation,

language, religion, political or other opinion, national or social origin, property, birth, or other status.[9] As affirmed by the UN, '*All* persons under any form of detention or imprisonment shall be treated in a humane manner and with respect for the inherent dignity of the human person'.[10]

The problem is that, despite the limitations on detention under international human rights law, practices of immigration detention continue to violate the rights of migrants. When States detain migrants, for example to facilitate removal to another State, the practical exclusion of migrants from equal enjoyment of their human rights often becomes severe. In this chapter, we aim to make visible the legal rights of detained migrants. Using international human rights law as a framework, the following sections outline the prohibition of arbitrary detention, obligations on States to implement procedural guarantees when they detain migrants, and obligations on States to ensure appropriate conditions of detention.

Prohibition of arbitrary detention

International law prohibits arbitrary detention.[11] The Human Rights Committee has repeatedly clarified that arbitrariness 'is not to be equated with "against the law", but must be interpreted more broadly to include elements of inappropriateness, injustice, lack of predictability and due process of law'.[12] To start, detention of migrants must only be undertaken on grounds 'clearly defined and exhaustively enumerated in legislation'.[13] The justificatory aims for detention established in law must be legitimate,[14] and each deprivation of liberty must be necessary and proportionate to achieving those aims.[15] Justifications must be particular to each individual case of detention.[16] Irregular entry alone is an insufficient justification, and other factors such as the likelihood of absconding or crimes being committed must be considered.[17] The conditions of legality, legitimacy, necessity, and proportionality must be met throughout the duration of detention, not only at the start.[18] To illustrate, if detention of a migrant for the purpose of removal becomes indefinite due to a decreasing prospect of the removal being effected, ongoing detention becomes arbitrary: 'The principle of proportionality requires that detention has a legitimate aim, which would not exist if there were no longer a real and tangible prospect of removal'.[19] Relatedly, detention must be for as short a period as possible.[20]

In a context where certain States criminalise irregular immigration, it is particularly important to stress, 'Detention must be the exception, not the rule'.[21] Detention is a measure of last resort, requiring that 'there were not less invasive means of achieving the same ends'.[22] To meet the requirements of necessity and proportionality, international law obliges States to consider less intrusive alternatives to detention,[23] which may include reporting requirements and restrictions on movement. The UN General Assembly has called on States to consider alternatives to detention in the context of protecting the human rights of migrants and ending arbitrary detention.[24]

Procedural guarantees

The avoidance of arbitrary detention to comply with international law is closely connected to the implementation of procedural guarantees when, as a last resort, States deprive a migrant of her or his liberty. Several sets of guidelines have been developed in this respect over the years.[25] Examples are given here of procedural guarantees, though space precludes full examination of all those applicable. To begin, detention must be ordered only by persons duly authorised to do so.[26] It must subsequently be reviewed periodically to ensure that it continues to be justified and has not become arbitrary.[27] Enumerating a maximum period of detention in law can be helpful in this regard.[28] When depriving migrants of their liberty through detention, States must notify them of the reasons for the measure in a form and language that they understand.[29] States must protect the detainee's right to access legal assistance and interpretation services, as well as to communicate with consular officials.[30] They must also ensure migrants' access to courts for judicial review of the lawfulness of detention, which is widely enshrined in human rights law as an important guarantee.[31] When detention is deemed unlawful, States must take steps to impose sanctions on those who acted in violation of national and international law.[32] Arbitrarily detained migrants are also entitled to effective remedies, including compensation.[33] States should review and reform detention laws which have a discriminatory and disproportionate effect on groups of migrants.[34] Respecting procedural guarantees such as these facilitates compliance with international human rights law.

Detention conditions

As well as procedural guarantees, there are obligations for States to provide adequate facilities for migrants in detention which respect their inherent dignity as human persons.[35] The OHCHR outlines the general principles for detention conditions that must be safeguarded, including[36] enjoyment of the highest attainable standard of physical and mental health;[37] basic standard of living including clothing, bedding, food, water, and space;[38] freedom from cruel, inhuman, or degrading punishment;[39] freedom to practise religion;[40] and a right to education.[41] Migrants who are held in detention for the purposes of immigration control have a different legal status from convicted prisoners or persons in pre-trial detention and must be held in separate, appropriate facilities.[42] There must be no arbitrary interference with correspondence from family, and migrants have a right to communicate with the outside world.[43] In addition, States are under the obligation to ensure complaints are heard and investigated by a competent authority.[44] Ensuring that facilities are monitored, including by allowing access by appropriate organisations, can help protect detainees from human rights abuses and deteriorating conditions.[45]

Special consideration must be given to the detention of vulnerable groups, such as women,[46] children,[47] and people with mental[48] and other disabilities.[49] The detention of children must be a measure of last resort, limited to the exceptional situations where the deprivation of minor's liberty would be in their best interest.[50] In response to the vulnerability of women migrant workers who are detained, CEDAW explains that States must take safeguarding measures to ensure protection from discrimination or gender-based violence and access to appropriate health-care services.[51] Finally, for migrants in detention, there must be effective access to asylum procedures.[52] Giving due consideration to appropriate conditions of detention can help to avoid human rights violations and respect the dignity of migrants.

torture victims! (handwritten margin note)

Conclusion

In conclusion, to ensure respect for the human rights of migrants, States should be aware of the following points when considering detention:

1   International law prohibits arbitrary detention;
2   When migrants are detained as a last resort, procedural guarantees must be implemented; and
3   Conditions of detention must be adequate to respect the human dignity of migrants deprived of their liberty.

Notes

1 A/71/L.1 para 33.
2 Costello, C., "Human Rights and the Elusive Universal Subject: Immigration Detention under International Human Rights and EU Law," *Indiana Journal of Global Legal Studies*, 19 (2012): 257–303, 258.
3 UN High Commissioner for Refugees (UNHCR), *Guidelines on the Applicable Criteria and Standards Relating to the Detention of Asylum-Seekers and Alternatives to Detention*, 2012, available at: http://www.refworld.org/docid/503489533b8. html [accessed 5 July 2017] p. 9.
4 A v Australia, Communication No.560/1993, UN Human Rights Committee (3 April 1997) para 9.3; UN General Assembly, Report to the Seventh Session of the Human Rights Council – Report of the Working Group on Arbitrary Detention (Report of the Working Group on Arbitrary Detention) (10 January 2008,

A/HRC/7/4) para 46; UN General Assembly, Report to the Thirteenth Session of the Human Rights Council – Report of the Working Group on Arbitrary Detention (18 January 2010, A/HRC/13/30) para 58

5 UN General Assembly (UNGA), Civil and Political Rights Covenant Article 9(1).

6 Civil and Political Rights Covenant Article 10; Migrant Workers Convention Article 17.

7 Ensured through judicial review, Civil and Political Rights Covenant Article 9(4); Migrant Workers Convention Article 16(8); UN General Assembly, Body of Principles for the Protection of All Persons under Any Form of Detention or Imprisonment (Body of Principles) (9 December 1988, A/RES/43/173) Principle 32(1).

8 Absolute ban on the use of torture under UN General Assembly, Convention against Torture Article 2; Civil and Political Rights Covenant Article 7.

9 Civil and Political Rights Covenant Articles 2(1) and 26; Migrant Workers Convention Article 7. See the introductory chapter in this publication

10 Body of Principles, Principle 1.

11 Universal Declaration Article 9; Civil and Political Rights Covenant Article 9(1); Child Rights Convention Article 37(b); Migrant Workers Convention Article 16(4); Human Rights Council (Commission as it then was), Report of the Special Rapporteur on the Human Rights of Migrants: Migrant Workers (30 December 2002, E/CN.4/2003/85) para 15: 'It is a fundamental principle of international law that no one should be subjected to arbitrary detention'.

12 Mukong v Cameroon, Communication No.458/1991, Human Rights Committee (21 July 1994) para 9.8; A v Australia, Communication No.560/1993, UN Human Rights Committee (3 April 1997) para 9.2; van Alphen v The Netherlands, Communication No.305/1988, Human Rights Committee (23 July 1990) para 5.8.

13 Report of the Working Group on Arbitrary Detention (2010), para 59; Civil and Political Rights Covenant Articles 9(1) and 12(3); Committee on the Rights of the Child, General Comment No. 6: Treatment of Unaccompanied and Separated Children Outside their Country of Origin (1 September 2005, CRC/GC/2005/6) para 61.

14 Migrant Workers Committee General Comment No. 2 on the rights of migrant workers in an irregular situation and members of their families (28 August 2013, CMW/C/GC/2) para 25; Human Rights Council, Report of the Working Group on Arbitrary Detention (24 December 2012, A/HRC/22/44) para 63; UN General Assembly, Report of the Special Rapporteur on the human rights of migrants, François Crépeau (2 April 2012, A/HRC/20/24) para 9: 'Legitimate objectives for detention are the same for migrants as they are for anyone else: when someone presents a risk of absconding from future legal proceedings or administrative processes or when someone presents a danger to their own or public security'.

15 Civil and Political Rights Covenant Article 12(3), van Alphen v The Netherlands, Communication No.305/1988, Human Rights Committee (23 July 1990) para 5.8: 'remand in custody pursuant to lawful arrest must not only be lawful but reasonable in all the circumstances. Further, remand in custody must be necessary in all the circumstances'.

16 A v Australia Communication No.560/1993, UN Human Rights Committee (3 April 1997) para 9.4; Shams v Australia Communication No. 1255, 1256, 1259, 1260, 1266, 1268, 1270, and 1288/2004, Human Rights Committee (20 July

2007), para 11: requiring 'grounds particular to the [individual] cases which would justify their continued detention'.

17 Human Rights Committee General Comment No. 35, Article 9 (Liberty and security of person) (16 December 2014, CCPR/C/GC/35) para 18; A v Australia, Communication No.560/1993, UN Human Rights Committee (3 April 1997) para 9.4: 'Without such factors detention may be considered arbitrary, even if entry was illegal'; Child Rights Committee General Comment No. 6: 'Detention cannot be justified solely on the basis of the child being unaccompanied or separated, or on their migratory or residence status, or lack thereof'; UNHCR Executive Committee, Detention of Refugees and Asylum-Seekers No. 44 (XXXVII) (13 October 1986) section (b).

18 C v Australia, Communication No.900/1999, Human Rights Committee (28 October 2002) para 8.2; Human Rights Committee General Comment No.35 para 18: 'The detention must be justified as reasonable, necessary and proportionate in the light of the circumstances and reassessed as it extends in time'.

19 Mr Mustafa Abdi v UK, Opinion No.45/2006, Working Group on Arbitrary Detention, paras 25 and 29; Report of the Working Group on Arbitrary Detention (2010), para 91: 'The principle of proportionality requires that detention has a legitimate aim, which would not exist if there were no longer a real and tangible prospect of removal'.

20 Child Rights Convention Article 37(b): 'Detention . . . shall be used only . . . for the shortest appropriate period of time'; D&E v Australia, Communication No.1050/2002, Human Rights Committee (11 July 2006) para 7.2: 'In order to avoid any characterization of arbitrariness, detention should not continue beyond the period for which a State party can provide appropriate justification'.

21 Report of the Working Group on Arbitrary Detention (2008), para 51.

22 C v Australia Communication No.900/1999, Human Rights Committee (28 October 2002) para 8.2; Child Rights Convention Article 37(b).

23 Report of the Working Group on Arbitrary Detention (2008), para 53; D&E v Australia Communication No.1050/2002, Human Rights Committee (11 July 2006), para 7.2; Shams v Australia, Communication No. 1255, 1256, 1259, 1260, 1266, 1268, 1270 & 1288/2004, Human Rights Committee (20 July 2007), para 7.2: 'The State party has not demonstrated that, in the light of each authors' particular circumstances, there were no less invasive means of achieving the same ends'.

24 UN General Assembly, Protection of migrants: resolution adopted by the General Assembly (25 February 2016, A/RES/70/147) para 4(a): 'Calls upon all States to respect the human rights and inherent dignity of migrants, to put an end to arbitrary arrest and detention and, in order to avoid excessive detention of irregular migrants, to review, where necessary, detention periods and to use alternatives to detention, where appropriate, including measures that have been successfully implemented by some States'.

25 Body of Principles, Human Rights Council (formerly Commission), Report of the Working Group on Arbitrary Detention (18 December 1998, E/CN.4/1999/63), paras 62–70; UNHCR Guidelines on Detention, Guideline 7; European Committee for the Prevention of Torture and Inhuman or Degrading Treatment or Punishment, Safeguards for irregular migrants deprived of their liberty (2009, CPT/Inf(2009)27) 35–44; Council of Europe, Twenty Guidelines on Forced Return (4 May 2005).

26 Civil and Political Rights Covenant Article 9(1); Migrant Workers Convention Article 16(4); Body of Principles, Principles 2 and 4.

27 A v. Australia para 9.4; Report of the Working Group on Arbitrary Detention (2010), para 61; Body of Principles, Principle 11(3): 'A judicial or other authority shall be empowered to review as appropriate the continuance of detention'.

28 Human Rights Council (formerly Commission), Report of the Working Group on Arbitrary Detention (28 December 1999, E/CN.4/2000/4) Deliberation No.5, Principle 7: 'A maximum period should be set by law'; UNHCR/OHCHR, Summary Conclusions from Global Roundtable on Alternatives to Detention of Asylum-Seekers, Refugees, Migrants and Stateless Persons (July 2011) para 2.

29 Civil and Political Rights Covenant Article 9(2); Migrant Workers Convention Article 16(5); Human Rights Committee General Comment No.35, paras 24–30; Report of the Working Group on Arbitrary Detention, (2010) Principle 8; Body of Principles, Principles 11(2), 13 and 14; Report of the Special Rapporteur on the Human Rights of Migrants, para 75(d).

30 Child Rights Convention Article 37(d); Migrant Workers Convention Articles 16(7) and 16(8); UN General Assembly Resolution 70/147 para 4(k); Body of Principles, Principles 11(1), 17, and 18; Human Rights Council (formerly Commission), Report of the UN Special Rapporteur on Torture and other Cruel, Inhuman or Degrading Treatment or Punishment (23 December 2003, E/CN.4/2004/56) para 43.

31 Civil and Political Rights Covenant Article 9(4): 'Anyone who is deprived of his liberty by arrest or detention shall be entitled to take proceedings before a court, in order that that court may decide without delay on the lawfulness of his detention and order his release if the detention is not lawful'; Migrant Workers Convention Article 16(8); Child Rights Convention Article 37(d); Body of Principles Principle 32(1); Human Rights Council (formerly Commission) Commission on Human Rights Resolution 2004/39: Arbitrary Detention (19 April 2004, E/CN.4/RES/2004/39) para 3(c).

32 UN General Assembly Resolution 70/147 para 4(h); Body of Principles, Principle 7(1): 'States should prohibit by law any act contrary to the rights and duties contained in these principles, make any such act subject to appropriate sanctions and conduct impartial investigations upon complaints'.

33 Universal Declaration Article 8: 'Everyone has the right to an effective remedy by the competent national tribunals for acts violating the fundamental rights granted him by the constitution or by law'; Civil and Political Rights Covenant Article 9(5); Migrant Workers Convention Article 16(9); Human Rights Council General Comment No.35, paras 49–52; D&E v Australia, Communication No.1050/2002, Human Rights Committee (11 July 2006) para 9.

34 CERD Committee, CERD General Recommendation XXXI on the Prevention of Racial Discrimination in the Administration and Functioning of the Criminal Justice System (2005) para 1(e): 'States parties should pay the greatest attention to the following possible indicators of racial discrimination . . . The number and percentage of persons belonging to those groups who are held in prison or preventive detention'; CEDAW Committee, General Recommendation No. 26 on women migrant workers (5 December 2008, CEDAW/C/2009/WP.1/R) para 26(j): 'They should review, eliminate or reform laws, regulations, or policies that result in a disproportionate number of women migrant workers being detained for migration-related reasons'.

35 Universal Declaration Article 1; Civil and Political Rights Covenant Article 10(1): 'All persons deprived of their liberty shall be treated with humanity and with respect for the inherent dignity of the human person'; Migrant Workers Convention Article 17(1); Body of Principles, Principle 1.

34   *Kathryn Allinson et al.*

36 OHCHR, *Human Rights and Prisons: A Pocketbook of International Human Rights Standards for Prison Officials*. New York and Geneva: United Nations, 2005.
37 Civil and Political Rights Covenant Article 12; Body of Principles, Principle 24; Social Rights Committee, General Comment No. 14: The Right to the Highest Attainable Standard of Health (11 August 2000, E/C.12/2000/4) para 34: 'States are under the obligation to respect the right to health by, inter alia, refraining from denying or limiting equal access for all persons, including prisoners or detainees, minorities, asylum-seekers and illegal immigrants, to preventive, curative and palliative health services'.
38 Universal Declaration, Article 25; Social Rights Covenant, Article 11; CRC, Article 27, UNHCR Guidelines on Detention, Guideline 8.
39 Universal Declaration Article 80, Civil and Political Rights Covenant Article 7, Convention against Torture Article 2.
40 Universal Declaration Article 18; Civil and Political Rights Covenant Article 18.
41 Universal Declaration Articles 26 and 27; Social Rights Covenant Article 13.
42 Civil and Political Rights Covenant Article 10, Migrant Workers Convention Article 17(3), Human Rights Committee General Comment No. 35 para 18, Report of the Working Group on Arbitrary Detention, Principle 9.
43 Universal Declaration Article 12, Migrant Workers Convention Article 17(5): 'During detention or imprisonment, migrant workers and members of their families shall enjoy the same rights as nationals to visits by members of their families'.
44 Civil and Political Rights Covenant Article 2, Convention against Torture Article 13, UNHCR Guidelines on Detention Guideline 8(xv).
45 Report of the Working Group on Arbitrary Detention, Principle 10.
46 CEDAW, e.g., Articles 2, 3, and 12; UN General Assembly, Declaration on the Elimination of Violence against Women 20 December 1993, A/RES/48/104) Articles 2 and 4.
47 Child Rights Convention Articles 3 and 37.
48 C v Australia Communication No.900/1999, Human Rights Committee (28 October 2002) para 8.4.
49 Hamilton v Jamaica, Communication No. 616/1995, Human Rights Committee (28 July 1999) para 8.2. See also International Commission of Jurists, Migration and International Human Rights Law: A Practitioners' Guide (Geneva, 2014) 205–207; OHCHR, Human Rights and Prisons.
50 Child Rights Convention Articles 3, 9, 22, and 37; Civil and Political Rights Covenant Articles 9 and 10; Child Rights Convention General Comment No. 6 para 63.
51 CEDAW Article 12 and General Recommendation 26 para 26j.
52 Universal Declaration Article 14.

5 Irregular status

Katharine T. Weatherhead

Migrants whose immigration status was irregular were denied access to shelter, food and other social benefits (including education and medical treatment). This included benefits for children.

CEC v Netherlands Complaint No. 90/2013 violation of the European Social Charter (equivalent rights to the Social Rights Covenant) European Committee of Social Rights decision 10 November 2014.

> We will consider reviewing our migration policies with a view to examining their possible unintended negative consequences.
> New York Declaration of the UN General Assembly
> 19 September 2016[1]

Just as migrants as a broad group are entitled to respect for their human rights, so too are the subset of migrants with irregular status. For the purpose of this chapter, migrants with irregular status are broadly defined as migrants who do not have the necessary approval or documentation to be in a State[2] and whose presence may or may not be known to State authorities. There are a variety of ways in which a migrant may come to have irregular status, including through clandestine entry into a State, overstaying the period approved in a visa or residence permit, breaching official terms of residence, or administrative delays in the processing of relevant documentation. The UN system has gradually adopted the terminology of irregularity as opposed to illegality.[3] This shift reflects the international consensus that the term 'illegal' to describe migrants is inaccurate and stigmatising. Regarding the terminology of illegality, the Special Rapporteur on the Human Rights of Migrants notes,

> The view and labelling of migrants among many stakeholders as "illegal" is counterproductive and is not supported by international law

illegal to be called something illegal

> ... A human being cannot be intrinsically illegal, and naming anyone as such dehumanizes that person. The conceptualization of irregular migrants as 'illegal' has undoubtedly played into the criminalization of migrants and thus to the practice of immigration detention. It has also had an impact on the general public's perception of migrants, legitimizing policies that are not in line with human rights guarantees and contributing to xenophobia, discrimination and violence.[4]

The dehumanisation of irregular migrants has a detrimental effect on the protection of their human rights. Though issues of irregularity are often discussed in relation to migrant workers, the aim of this chapter is to highlight that international human rights law guarantees a wide set of rights to irregular migrants in all contexts. The following paragraphs discuss the scope of irregular migrants' rights under international human rights law, the limitations to differential treatment, and the ways in which human rights law impacts upon State measures to manage migration.

Human rights regardless of status

The first point to note is that, under international law, irregular status does not deprive a migrant of her or his human rights. The foundational precept of international human rights law is that human rights are accorded to everyone equally.[5] The universality of human rights is supported by the principle of non-discrimination, which precludes differential enjoyment of human rights based on 'distinction of any kind, such as race, colour, sex, language, religion, political or other opinion, national or social origin, property, birth or other status'.[6] Migrants with irregular status are accordingly entitled to equal protection of their human rights, such as freedom from torture,[7] the right to family life,[8] the right to health,[9] the right to education,[10] and the right of access to courts.[11]

The UN Treaty Bodies explicitly affirm that the human rights treaties apply equally to migrants with irregular status.[12] For example, the Committee on the Elimination of Discrimination Against Women 'emphasizes that *all categories of women migrants* fall within the scope of the obligations of States . . . and must be protected against all forms of discrimination by the Convention [on the Elimination of Discrimination Against Women]'.[13] Similarly, the Committee on the Rights of the Child affirms that

> the enjoyment of rights stipulated in the Convention [on the Rights of the Child] is not limited to children who are citizens of a State party and must therefore, if not explicitly stated otherwise in the Convention, also be available to all children – including asylum-seeking, refugee

and migrant children – *irrespective of their nationality, immigration status or statelessness.*[14]

As a further illustration, the Committee on the Elimination of Racial Discrimination recommends that States '[e]nsure that legislative guarantees against racial discrimination apply to non-citizens *regardless of their immigration status*'.[15] Whether a migrant's status is irregular or regular, States are obliged to protect their human rights.

Limits to differential treatment

The second point to note is that international human rights law contains only limited exceptions to the prohibition of differential treatment of non-citizens, including non-citizens with irregular status. In the Civil and Political Rights Covenant, distinctions between citizens and non-citizens arise in the case of two groups of rights. One is a set of political rights to participate in public affairs, vote, be elected, and have equal access to public service, which need only be guaranteed to citizens.[16] The other is a set of free movement rights, principally 'the right to liberty of movement and freedom to choose his residence', which need only be guaranteed to persons lawfully within State territory.[17] In the International Covenant on Economic, Social and Cultural Rights (the Social Rights Covenant), developing countries are allowed a measure of discretion in the extent to which they guarantee economic rights to migrants.[18] However, as with any exception in human rights law, this provision is to be interpreted narrowly.[19] Additionally, the International Convention on the Elimination of Racial Discrimination stipulates that the 'Convention shall not apply to distinctions, exclusions, restrictions or preferences made by a State . . . between citizens and non-citizens'.[20] Written in the context of aiming to eliminate racial discrimination, this latter provision recognises that States can and do treat citizens and non-citizens differently in certain instances, such as in their rights to vote and move freely in State territory, as long as the distinctions in treatment do not undermine the general principle of non-discrimination.[21] There are thus few exceptions in international human rights law to the rule of equal treatment of citizens and non-citizens, including those with irregular status.

Furthermore, the principle of non-discrimination limits the use of any of these exceptional provisions which allow for differential treatment. Distinctions in treatment 'may be made only if they are to serve a legitimate State objective and are proportional to the achievement of that objective'.[22] Irregular status does not nullify the State's obligation to ensure that differential treatment of migrants is non-discriminatory, legitimate, and proportionate. State action must be scrutinised to ensure that any differential treatment between irregular migrants and other persons complies with the limits set by international law.

Legally compliant migration management

Finally, States must comply with their human rights obligations when managing migration, whether it be regular or irregular migration.[23] States retain sovereign authority to regulate the entry and stay of migrants, and international human rights law does not contain an explicit right to regularisation of migration status.[24] However, measures to regulate migration must conform to the legal framework which enshrines the equal enjoyment of everyone to human rights, both in law and in practice.[25] The legal framework applies at the stages of entry and removal of migrants, as well as during their stay within a State's jurisdiction. Regarding entry and removal, States must protect each migrant's rights at borders.[26] State duties include the obligation not to return a migrant to a country where her or his life, liberty, or security may be jeopardised.[27] States must also comply with the prohibition of arbitrary detention and the obligation to consider less intrusive alternatives to detention, particularly in cases where legal or practical barriers to removal would make detention of irregular migrants indefinite in duration.[28]

As well as during entry and removal, human rights guarantees are applicable to migrants while they remain within a State's jurisdiction. The example of reporting requirements illustrates the challenges that migration management can pose to effective protection of migrants during irregular stay. Requirements placed upon service providers to report irregular status to immigration authorities, at times linked to the criminalisation of irregular entry or stay, can be detrimental to irregular migrants' ability to access their human rights. Under international law, '[p]rimary education shall be compulsory and available free to all',[29] including irregularly present migrant children.[30] If educational institutions are required to report migration status to State authorities, migrant children with irregular status may be unable to realise their right to primary education out of fear of detention or deportation. Similar challenges arise when health-care providers are required to report irregular status, though the Committee on Economic, Social and Cultural Rights affirms that

> States are under the obligation to respect the right to health by, inter alia, refraining from denying or limiting equal access for all persons, including prisoners or detainees, minorities, asylum seekers and illegal immigrants, to preventive, curative and palliative health services.[31]

Considering that measures of migration management risk worsening the precarity associated with irregular status, it is important for States to ensure that they meet their obligations under international law to protect the human rights of irregular migrants at all times during their entry, removal, and stay.

Conclusion

In sum, three points of international law should be borne in mind when States consider the position of irregular migrants:

1 Migrants are entitled to human rights regardless of their irregular status;
2 International human rights law prohibits differential treatment of non-citizens, including irregular migrants, subject to limited exceptions; and
3 Measures of migration management must not jeopardise protection of, and effective access to, the human rights of irregular migrants.

Notes

1 A/71/L.1 para 45.
2 International human rights law does not define the term 'irregular migrant', but Article 5 of Migrant Workers Convention defines migrant workers in an irregular situation as migrant workers who are not 'authorized to enter, to stay and to engage in a remunerated activity in the State of employment pursuant to the law of that State and to international agreements to which that State is a party'.
3 For a notable early call to use the terms 'undocumented' or 'irregular', see UN General Assembly, Measures to ensure the human rights and dignity of all migrant workers (9 December 1975, Res 3449 (XXX)), para 2; for a recent comment from a treaty body, see the Migrant Workers Committee, General Comment No. 2 on the rights of migrant workers in an irregular situation and members of their families (28 August 2013, CMW/C/GC/2) para 4.
4 UN General Assembly, Report of the Special Rapporteur on the human rights of migrants (4 August 2016, A/71/285) para 31.
5 Universal Declaration Article 1. See also the introductory chapter in this publication.
6 Universal Declaration Article 2, Civil and Political Rights Covenant Article 2(1), Social Rights Covenant Article 2(2), Child Rights Convention Article 2. Particularly relevant to migrants with irregular status is the prohibition of discrimination on the grounds of race, national origin, and 'other status'.
7 Universal Declaration Article 5; Convention against Torture Article 2, Civil and Political Rights Covenant Article 7.
8 Universal Declaration Article 16, Civil and Political Rights Covenant Article 23.
9 Universal Declaration Article 25, Social Rights Covenant Article 12.
10 Universal Declaration Article 26, Social Rights Covenant Article 13.
11 Universal Declaration Article 10, Civil and Political Rights Covenant Article 14, Human Rights Committee, General Comment No. 32, Article 14: Right to equality before courts and tribunals and to fair trial (23 August 2007, CCPR/C/GC/32) para 9: 'The right of access to courts and tribunals and equality before them is not limited to citizens of States parties, but must also be available to all

individuals, regardless of nationality or statelessness, or whatever their status, whether asylum seekers, refugees, migrant workers, unaccompanied children or other persons, who may find themselves in the territory or subject to the jurisdiction of the State party'.

12 Social Rights Committee, General Comment No. 20: Non-discrimination in Economic, Social and Cultural Rights (2 July 2009, E/C.12/GC/20) para 30: 'The Covenant rights apply to everyone including non-nationals, such as refugees, asylum-seekers, stateless persons, migrant workers and victims of international trafficking, regardless of legal status and documentation'; Human Rights Committee, General Comment no. 31 [80], The Nature of the General Legal Obligation Imposed on States Parties to the Covenant (26 May 2004, CCPR/C/21/Rev.1/Add.13) para 10: 'States Parties are required by Article 2, paragraph 1, to respect and to ensure the Covenant rights to all persons who may be within their territory and to all persons subject to their jurisdiction'; Human Rights Committee, General Comment No. 15: The Position of Aliens Under the Covenant (11 April 1986).

13 Committee on the Elimination of Discrimination Against Women, General Recommendation No. 26 on women migrant workers (5 December 2008, CEDAW/C/2009/WP.1/R) para 4, emphasis added.

14 Committee on the Rights of the Child, General Comment No. 6: Treatment of Unaccompanied and Separated Children Outside their Country of Origin (1 September 2005, CRC/GC/2005/6) para 12; UN General Assembly, Migrant children and adolescents (11 February 2015, A/RES/69/187) para 5, emphasis added.

15 Committee on the Elimination of Racial Discrimination, General Recommendation No. 30 on Discrimination Against Non-Citizens (1 October 2002) para 7, emphasis added.

16 Civil and Political Rights Covenant Article 25.

17 Civil and Political Rights Covenant Articles 12(1) and 13. These articles do not, however, allow for the arbitrary detention of migrants with irregular status, which is prohibited under international law: Universal Declaration Article 9, Civil and Political Rights Covenant Article 9(1), Child Rights Convention Article 37(b). See also the chapter on immigration detention in this publication.

18 Social Rights Covenant Article 2(3): 'Developing countries, with due regard to human rights and their national economy, may determine to what extent they would guarantee the economic rights recognized in the present Covenant to non-nationals'.

19 The drafting history of this provision also points to a narrow interpretation, see UN Commission on Human Rights, The Limburg Principles on the Implementation of the International Covenant on Economic, Social and Cultural Rights (8 January 1987, E/CN.4/1987/17) paras 42–44.

20 ICERD Article 1(2).

21 CERD Committee General Recommendation No. 30 para 2: 'Article 1, paragraph 2 . . . should not be interpreted to detract in any way from the rights and freedoms recognized and enunciated in particular in the Universal Declaration of Human Rights, the International Covenant on Economic, Social and Cultural Rights and the International Covenant on Civil and Political Rights'; ICERD Article 1(3): 'Nothing in this Convention may be interpreted as affecting in any way the legal provisions of States parties concerning nationality, citizenship or naturalization, provided that such provisions do not discriminate against any particular nationality', emphasis added.

22 UN Sub-commission on the Promotion and Protection of Human Rights, The Rights of Non-citizens: Final Report of the Special Rapporteur, David Weissbrodt (26 May 2003, E/CN.4/Sub.2/2003/23) para 1; Human Rights Committee, General Comment No. 18: Non-discrimination (10 November 1989) para 13; Social Rights Committee General Comment No. 20 para 13; CERD General Recommendation No. 30 para 4.

23 UN General Assembly, Protection of Migrants (25 February 2016, A/RES/70/147) 4: 'Stressing the importance of all regulations and laws regarding irregular migration, at all levels of government, being in accordance with the obligations of States under international law, including international human rights law'

24 Human Rights Committee General Comment No. 15, para 5: 'The Covenant does not recognize the right of aliens to enter or reside in the territory of a State party'; Migrant Workers Convention, Article 35. See also the chapter on rights of residence in this publication.

25 Human Rights Committee General Comment No. 15, para 4: 'In their reports States parties should give attention to the position of aliens, both under their law and in actual practice'. The obligation to equally protect human rights in law as well as in effect is also a fundamental part of the non-discrimination principle. See, e.g., Social Rights Committee General Comment No. 20, para 7; Human Rights Committee General Comment No. 18, para 7.

26 See Chapter 3 on rights at the border; see also OHCHR, Recommended Principles and Guidelines on Human Rights at International Borders (2014).

27 This obligation is enshrined in the principle of non-refoulement: Convention against Torture Article 3; Civil and Political Rights Covenant Articles 6 and 7; Refugee Convention Article 33(1); Human Rights Committee, General Comment No. 20: Article 7 (Prohibition of Torture, or Other Cruel, Inhuman or Degrading Treatment or Punishment) (10 March 1992) para 9; Human Rights Committee General Comment No. 31, para 12.

28 See Chapter 4 on immigration detention; see also Universal Declaration Article 9, Civil and Political Rights Covenant Article 9(1), Child Rights Convention Article 37(b), Human Rights Council, Human Rights of Migrants (6 October 2010, HRC A/HRC/RES/15/16) para 8: 'Calls upon all States to respect the human rights and the inherent dignity of migrants and to put an end to arbitrary arrest and detention and, where necessary, to review detention periods in order to avoid excessive detention of irregular migrants, and to adopt, where applicable, alternative measures to detention'.

29 Social Rights Covenant Article 13(2).

30 Social Rights Committee, General Comment No. 13: The Right to Education (8 December 1999, E/C.12/1999/10) para 34: 'The principle of non-discrimination extends to all persons of school age residing in the territory of a State party, including non-nationals, and irrespective of their legal status'.

31 Social Rights Committee, General Comment No. 14: The Right to the Highest Attainable Standard of Health (11 August 2000, E/C.12/2000/4) para 34; Social Rights Committee, General Comment No. 19: The right to social security (4 February 2008, E/C.12/GC/19) para 37: 'All persons, irrespective of their nationality, residency or immigration status, are entitled to primary and emergency medical care'; Migration Workers Committee General Comment No. 2 paras 72–4.

6 Rights of residence, termination of residence and in respect of removal

Valeria Vita

A migrant lawfully resided in a host country for 14 years, when he decided to visit his home country for six months. On his return, he was refused entry to the host state without being given any explanation. The authorities had received some information about the migrant being involved in some unspecified 'illegal activity' in his home country but gave no detail or reasons to him.

Ilyasov v Kazakhstan Human Rights Committee violation of Civil and Political Rights Covenant Communication No. 2009/2010 23 July 2014.

> We will continue to protect the human rights and fundamental freedoms of all persons, in transit and after arrival.
> New York Declaration of the UN General Assembly
> 19 September 2016[1]

International law does not recognize to all migrants a right to enter or reside in the territory of a country different from their own. Certain categories of migrants have this right on the basis of bilateral or multilateral agreements, such as the rules on free movement within Mercosur or the European Union (EU). Nonetheless, once a migrant is legally in a State, he or she enjoys the right to liberty of movement and freedom to choose his or her residence. Furthermore, even so-called irregular migrants are protected by a multitude of safeguards (see the previous chapter). Everybody has the right to leave any country, the right to return to one's country and is protected against the risk of arbitrary or collective removal. Finally, even if international law does not explicitly recognize a right to enter a State, this may be inferred, in certain circumstances, by other considerations, such as international protection, non-discrimination and prohibition of inhuman treatment including protection of family life depending on the situation (see Chapter 9).

The right to liberty of movement and freedom to choose a residence

Article 13(1) of the 1948 the Universal Declaration states, 'Everyone has the *right to freedom of movement and residence* within the borders of each State'. During the *travaux préparatoires* of the Universal Declaration, several countries proposed to amend this article, specifying that this right should only apply to the State of which a person is a national.[2] These amendments were not accepted because they would have meant that migrants admitted into a country would not have enjoyed the same rights as the citizens of that country. The representative of Haiti emphasised that everyone should be entitled to settle in the country of his or her choice, though not all the representatives agreed.[3] Indeed, it is at the discretion of the State to grant entry to its territory to migrants, and Article 13 only applies to migrants authorized to reside in the country. This right is also recognized in Article 5(d)(i) of the International Convention on the Elimination of All Forms of Racial Discrimination.

Therefore, Article 12(3) of the Civil and Political Rights Covenant is more precise and specifies that the right to liberty of movement and freedom to choose his or her residence is recognized to everyone lawfully within the territory of a State. It states that any permissible restriction to this right must be 'provided by law, [be] necessary to protect national security, public order (*ordre public*), public health or morals or the rights and freedoms of others, and [be] consistent with the other rights recognized in the present Covenant'. This means that once an alien is lawfully on the territory, his freedom of movement may only be restricted admitting that its limitations do not nullify the principle of liberty of movement, are determined by the requirement of necessity and are consistent with the other rights recognized in the Covenant. The Human Rights Committee has elaborated the meaning of this provision, underlining the importance 'that States parties indicate in their reports the circumstances in which they treat aliens differently from their nationals in this regard, and how they justify this difference in treatment'.[4] The grounds of permissible restrictions stated in paragraph 2 apply to all the provisions of Article 12; for example, the consistency with all other rights guaranteed in the Covenant will determine, in relation to paragraph 1, that any restriction to the freedom of movement must be compatible with the fundamental principles of equality and non-discrimination, and thus not distinguish on the basis of national origin, or other status; in relation to paragraph 4, 'a State party cannot, by restraining an alien or deporting him to a third country, arbitrarily prevent his return to his own country'.[5]

The prohibition of arbitrary and collective removal

Under Article 13 of the Civil and Political Rights Covenant, the prohibition of *arbitrary removal* is a fundamental provision which applies only to migrants (not citizens) who regularly stay within the territory of the State. It provides that

> an alien lawfully in the territory of a State Party to the present Covenant may be expelled therefrom only in pursuance of a decision reached in accordance with law and shall, except where compelling reasons of national security otherwise require, be allowed to submit the reasons against his removal and to have his case reviewed by, and be represented for the purpose before, the competent authority or a person or persons especially designated by the competent authority.

In General Comment 15, the Human Rights Committee clarified three points on Article 13: firstly, this provision is applicable to all procedures concerning the obligatory departure of an alien, regardless of the term used to describe them; secondly, the specification that an alien who is to be expelled can choose to leave to any country that agrees to take him back; finally, even if this article can only be applied to migrants who are lawfully on the territory of a State, any decision regarding the removal of people whose legality of stay is in dispute must be in accordance with Article 13.[6]

Even though the Civil and Political Rights Covenant does not directly address arbitrariness and does not provide for an explicit prohibition of *collective removal*, the Human Rights Committee explained,

> Article 13 directly regulates only the procedure and not the substantive grounds for expulsion. However, by allowing only those carried out 'in pursuance of a decision reached in accordance with law', its purpose is clearly to prevent arbitrary expulsions. Moreover, as it entitles each alien to a decision in his own case, collective or mass expulsions would also be incompatible with Article 13. This understanding, in the opinion of the Committee, is confirmed by further provisions concerning the right to submit reasons against expulsion and to have the decision reviewed by and to be represented before the competent authority or someone designated by it. An alien must be given full facilities for pursuing his remedy against expulsion so that this right will in all the circumstances of his case be an effective one. The principles of Article 13 relating to appeal against expulsion and the entitlement to review by a competent authority may only be departed from when 'compelling reasons of national security' so require. Discrimination may not be made between different categories of aliens in the application of article 13.[7]

While the Civil and Political Rights Covenant prohibits arbitrary (and implicitly collective) expulsion only for migrants who are lawfully in the territory of the State, the Migrant Workers Convention contains a number of rights for both regular and irregular migrant workers and members of their families (Part III Human Rights of All Migrant Workers and Members of their Families). For example, Article 22 prohibits arbitrary and collective expulsion for all migrant workers and members of their families regardless of their regular status.

Specific concern arises in respect of stateless persons for whom removal from the State is practically very difficult. UNHCR in its Handbook on the Protection of Stateless Persons has stated,

> 111 Routine detention of individuals seeking protection on the grounds of statelessness is arbitrary. Statelessness, by its very nature, severely restricts access to basic identity and travel documents that nationals normally possess.[8]

Article 22 of the Migrant Workers Convention prohibits arbitrary and collective removal, as it affirms that each removal order must be taken by the competent authority in accordance with law and after an individual assessment. According to the Committee on the Protection of the Rights of All Migrant Workers and Members of Their Families, States parties must provide

> sufficient guarantees to ensure that the personal circumstances of each migrant worker are genuinely and individually taken into account. This obligation extends to all spaces over which a State party exercises effective control, which may include vessels on the high seas.[9]

Furthermore, Article 22 affirms a variety of procedural safeguards, including the right to receive any communication in a language one can understand, to have a written and reasoned decision and the opportunity to submit arguments against the action. In particular, this means that 'while a stay of decision does not regularize the status of the person concerned for the time of the proceedings, it prevents the State party from expelling him or her before a final decision is rendered'.[10] According to Article 83 of the Migrant Workers Convention, States parties must provide an effective remedy against a negative decision, including the right to legal assistance and the assistance of an interpreter (see further in Chapter 11).

The right to leave any country and to return to his or her country

Regardless of the lawful or otherwise status of a migrant within the territory and besides the Migrant Workers Convention, there are some rights and guarantees connected to residence, which are recognized to irregular migrants (see also Chapter 5). Two of them are grounded in the Universal Declaration, Article 13(2), according to which 'Everyone has the *right to leave any country, including his own, and to return to his country*'. The same rights are reaffirmed in Article 12(2, 4) of the Civil and Political Rights Covenant and in Article 5(d)(ii) of the International Convention on the Elimination of All Forms of Racial Discrimination. Not only does the letter of this provision deliberately state 'everyone', but the Human Rights Committee has specified that 'everyone' precisely means that also 'an alien being legally expelled from the country is likewise entitled to elect the State of destination, subject to the agreement of that State'.[11] The agreement of the State is only required if the State of destination elected by the expelled individual is not his national one, as all States are bond by a duty to readmit their own nationals. The extent of this duty is not entirely clear: if it is inferred from the right to return to his or her own country, it will operate only in the presence of the national's will to return. However, the existence of such a general obligation is accepted by some doctrine as a norm of customary law.[12] A likewise duty to readmit foreigners is much more controversial and cannot be considered as general international law. Nonetheless, it must be reminded what the Human Rights Committee held in this regard: the necessity of a broader interpretation of the term 'his own country', which may embrace other categories of long-term residents[13] and thus appears to extend the duty of States to readmit other countries nationals.

Connected to the right to leave any country, the Human Rights Committee also stated,

> Since international travel usually requires appropriate documents, in particular a passport, the right to leave a country must include the right to obtain the necessary travel documents. The issuing of passports is normally incumbent on the State of nationality of the individual. The refusal by a State to issue a passport or prolong its validity for a national residing abroad may deprive this person of the right to leave the country of residence and to travel elsewhere. It is no justification for the State to claim that its national would be able to return to its territory without a passport.[14]

In relation to this statement, it is significant to note that what is also at stake here is the importance of the right to legal recognition; in other words, the possession of identity documents, which, representing evidence of a certain status, entitle individuals to all rights related to that status. This right (which is further analysed in Chapter 1) was firstly acknowledged in Article 6 of the Universal Declaration and Article 16 of the Civil and Political Rights Covenant and itemized in the right of a child to be registered immediately after birth, as stated in Article 24(2) Civil and Political Rights Covenant and Article 29 Migrant Workers Convention, as far as it concerns children of migrant workers. The Human Rights Council has indeed affirmed that

> in adulthood birth certificates may be required to obtain formal sector employment, to buy or prove the right to inherit property, to vote and to obtain a passport. Non-registration therefore undermines fulfilment of the rights of all persons, inter alia, to vote (Civil and Political Rights Covenant Article 25), the right to a nationality (the Universal Declaration, Article 15) and the right of everyone to be free to leave any country, and not be arbitrarily deprived of the right to enter their own country (Civil and Political Rights Covenant Article 12).[15]

Other considerations

As mentioned earlier, other considerations may determine the right of migrants to enter or reside in a country: these are international protection, protection of family life, non-discrimination and prohibition of inhuman treatment (*non-refoulement*). International protection specifically concerns asylum seekers, subsidiary protection holders and refugees, and its assessment is thus not specifically relevant for the purposes of this paper. Protection of family life is examined in Chapter 9.

Considerations related to non-discrimination and *non-refoulement* are especially significant in relation to removal. Despite the fact that the Convention on the Elimination of Racial Discrimination does not contain any specific provisions on removal, the Committee on the Elimination of Racial Discrimination focused on this issue in its General Recommendation 30, where it affirmed that

> laws concerning deportation or other forms of removal of non-citizens from the jurisdiction of the State party [must] not discriminate in purpose or effect among non-citizens on the basis of race, colour or ethnic or national origin, and that non-citizens have equal access to effective remedies, including the right to challenge expulsion orders, and are allowed effectively to pursue such remedies.[16]

The principle of *non-refoulement* – which is part of customary as well as treaty law – is the cornerstone of refugee law. However, it can be applied to all migrants. While Article 33 of the Refugee Convention applies only to refugees, the Convention against Torture has broadened its scope. Article 3 of Convention against Torture states,

> No State Party shall expel, return ('*refouler*') or extradite a person to another State where there are substantial grounds for believing that he would be in danger of being subjected to torture. For the purpose of determining whether there are such grounds, the competent authorities shall take into account all relevant considerations including, where applicable, the existence in the State concerned of a consistent pattern of gross, flagrant or mass violations of human right.

This provision expressly prohibits the removal of any migrant to a country where he or she could be subjected to inhumane or degrading treatment. The Committee against Torture elaborated on this provision in its General Comment 1, where it also addressed the so-called onward refoulement, stating,

> The Committee is of the view that the phrase 'another State' in Article 3 refers to the State to which the individual concerned is being expelled, returned or extradited, as well as to any State to which the author may subsequently be expelled, returned or extradited.[17]

The principle of *non-refoulement* has been reaffirmed by the Committee on the Protection of the Rights of All Migrant Workers and Members of Their Families, which stated that it is derived from those provisions which affirm the right to life and the prohibition of torture and cruel, inhuman or degrading treatment or punishment for all migrant workers and members of their families (Articles 9 and 10 of Migrant Workers Convention).[18]

Conclusion

In conclusion, when the liberty of movement of migrants is at stake, States must remember the following:

1 No one, regardless their migration status, shall be prevented from leaving a country or returning to their own country;
2 Anyone, once lawfully within the territory of a country, shall be free to move within the borders and choose where to reside; and
3 Removal shall be carried out only following the conclusion of a procedure prescribed by law and only after an individual assessment of the situation of the migrant.

Notes

1 A/71/L.1 para 26.
2 A/C.3/284/Rev.1 16 October 1948.
3 Mrs. Roosevelt, representative of the USA, noted, 'Economic considerations had, however, forced certain countries to take legal measures restricting immigration. Those measures were well known and generally accepted. A declaration of human rights should not contain principles the application of which was rendered impossible by existing circumstances' A/C.3/SR.120 2 November 1948.
4 Civil and Political Rights Committee 'General Comment No. 27 (67) on freedom of movement' (2 Nov 1999) UN Doc CCPR/C/21/Rev.1/Add.9 para 4.
5 Civil and Political Rights Committee 'General Comment No. 15: The Position of Aliens under the Covenant' (11 Apr 1986) para 8.
6 Ibid. para 9.
7 Ibid. para 10.
8 UNHCR Handbook on the Protection of Stateless Persons June 2014.
9 Migrant Workers Convention, General Comment No. 2 on the rights of migrant workers in an irregular situation and members of their families (28 Aug 2013) UN Doc CMW/C/GC/2 para 51.
10 Ibid. para 53.
11 Civil and Political Rights Committee General Comment No. 27 (67) on freedom of movement (2 Nov 1999) UN Doc CCPR/C/21/Rev.1/Add.9 para 8.
12 Hailbronner, K., 'Readmission Agreements and the Obligation of States under Public International Law to Readmit Their Own and Foreign Nationals', *Zeitschrift für ausländisches öffentliches Recht und Völkerrecht*, 57 (1997, pp. 1–49).
13 Civil and Political Rights Committee General Comment No. 27 (67) on freedom of movement (2 Nov 1999) UN Doc CCPR/C/21/Rev.1/Add.9 para 20.
14 Ibid. para 9.
15 Human Rights Council, 'Strengthening Policies and Programmes for Universal Birth Registration and Vital Statistics Development. Report of the High Commissioner for Human Rights' (1 Jul 2016) UN Doc A/HRC/33/22 para 8.
16 Committee on the Elimination of Racial Discrimination, 'General Recommendation No. 30 on Discrimination against Non-citizens' (2004) UN Doc CERD/C/64/Misc.11/rev.3 para 25.
17 CAT, 'General Comment No. 1: Implementation of Article 3 of the Convention in the Context of Article 22 (Refoulement and Communications)' (21 Nov 1997) UN Doc A/53/44 para 2.
18 CMW, 'General Comment No. 2 on the Rights of Migrant Workers in an Irregular Situation and Members of Their Families' (28 Aug 2013) UN Doc CMW/C/GC/2 para 50.

7 The economic, social and cultural rights of migrants[1]

Claude Cahn

Soldiers retired from an army had their pensions frozen because they were migrants (including those who had returned to their country of origin). They claimed discrimination in respect of their economic rights.

Ibrahima Gueye et al. v. France, Human Rights Committee, violation of the Civil and Political Rights Covenant Communication No. 196/1985, UN Doc. CCPR/C/35/D/196/1985 (1989).

> We recall that our obligations under international law prohibit discrimination of any kind on the basis of race, colour, sex, language, religion, political or other opinion, national or social origin, property, birth or other status. Yet in many parts of the world we are witnessing, with great concern, increasingly xenophobic and racist responses to refugees and migrants.
>
> New York Declaration of the UN General Assembly 19 September 2016[2]

International law has grappled with questions of obligations of States to respect, protect and fulfil the economic, social and cultural rights of migrants, as well as to design policies to secure migrant inclusion on the basis of equal dignity. As in so many other areas, the answers provided by international human rights law can guide the policymaker in these areas, as the guideposts are now fairly well established, notwithstanding some grey areas. The paragraphs that follow set out a broad scope of the acquis as currently understood in these areas.

As a starting point, the international human rights treaties guarantee rights to 'everyone', without regard to citizenship, in keeping with our global commitment that all persons are born equal in dignity and in rights. In the area of economic, social and cultural rights, Article 2(2) of the Social Rights Covenant obliges each State Party 'to guarantee that the rights enunciated in the present Covenant will be exercised without discrimination of any kind as to race, colour, sex, language, religion, political or other opinion, national or social origin, property, birth or other status'.

Three categories of obligations

As a general matter, the obligations under the Social Rights Covenant are deemed to fall into three categories: obligations to respect, obligations to protect and obligations to fulfil. The respect doctrine holds that States shall not actively violate the economic, social and cultural rights of persons; the protect doctrine holds that States shall adopted laws, policies and other measures which ensure that persons shall not suffer violations by any party, including by private or other non-state actors; and the fulfil doctrine holds that States have positive obligations to 'take steps' which are deliberate and targeted to the swiftest possible advancement of the implementation of economic, social and cultural rights.[3] The Social Rights Committee has, over the course of the period from the early 1990s to the present, undertaken extensive efforts to elaborate the meaning and normative content of substantive rights set out under the Social Rights Covenant treaty, in particular under its General Comments.[4]

Prohibited discrimination or difference of treatment

A key milestone in advancing understanding of the legitimacy or illegitimacy of differences of treatment based on nationality is the Social Rights Committee General Comment 20 on Non-discrimination in Economic, Social and Cultural Rights, adopted in 2009. In General Comment 20, the Social Rights Committee sets out that, 'the preamble, Articles 1, paragraph 3, and 55, of the Charter of the UN and Article 2, paragraph 1, of the Universal Declaration prohibit discrimination in the enjoyment of economic, social and cultural rights'.[5] The Social Rights Committee proceeds to clarify the primary term of relevance explicitly included in the Social Rights Covenant treaty as a ground of proscribed different treatment – 'national or social origin' – as follows:

> 'National origin' refers to a person's State, nation, or place of origin. Due to such personal circumstances, individuals and groups of individuals may face systemic discrimination in both the public and private sphere in the exercise of their Covenant rights. 'Social origin' refers to a person's inherited social status, which is discussed more fully below in the context of 'property' status, descent-based discrimination under 'birth' and 'economic and social status'.[6]

In addition, the Social Rights Committee read into the term 'other status' a number of other proscribed grounds, including 'nationality':

> The ground of nationality should not bar access to Covenant rights, e.g., all children within a State, including those with an undocumented status, have a right to receive education and access to adequate food and affordable health care. The Covenant rights apply to everyone including migrants, such as refugees, asylum-seekers, stateless persons, migrant workers and victims of international trafficking, regardless of legal status and documentation.[7]

The Social Rights Committee deemed that the ban on discrimination based on nationality under Social Rights Covenant was

> without prejudice to the application of Article 2(3) of the Covenant, which states: 'Developing countries, with due regard to human rights and their national economy, may determine to what extent they would guarantee the economic rights recognized in the present Covenant to non-nationals'.[8]

Closely linked to the question of discrimination based on national origin is the question of discrimination on grounds of birth. As concerns 'birth', the Social Rights Committee elaborates that

> discrimination based on birth is prohibited and Article 10(3) specifically states, for example, that special measures should be taken on behalf of children and young persons 'without any discrimination for reasons of parentage'. Distinctions must therefore not be made against those who are born out of wedlock, born of stateless parents or are adopted or constitute the families of such persons. The prohibited ground of birth also includes *descent*, especially on the basis of caste and analogous systems of inherited status. States parties should take steps, for instance, to prevent, prohibit and eliminate discriminatory practices directed against members of descent-based communities and act against dissemination of ideas of superiority and inferiority on the basis of descent.[9]

Several other grounds named explicitly in Social Rights Covenant Article 2(2) are also of direct relevance to migrants. These include 'race and colour', 'language' and 'religion':

Race

As concerns 'race and colour', the potential overlap between questions related to purported race, colour or ethnicity on the one hand, and nationality or national origin on the other, has taxed international law, particularly as concerns rights of entry onto the territory and establishment, and these dilemmas are inscribed into international treaty law, in particular the ICERD. For the purposes of the law of economic, social and cultural rights, the Social Rights Committee has elaborated as follows:

> Discrimination on the basis of 'race and colour', which includes an individual's ethnic origin, is prohibited by the Covenant as well as by other treaties including the International Convention on the Elimination of Racial Discrimination. The use of the term 'race' in the Covenant or the present General Comment does not imply the acceptance of theories which attempt to determine the existence of separate human races.[10,11]

Language

On language, the Social Rights Committee provides the following:

> Discrimination on the basis of language or regional accent is often closely linked to unequal treatment on the basis of national or ethnic origin. Language barriers can hinder the enjoyment of many Covenant rights, including the right to participate in cultural life as guaranteed by Article 15 of the Covenant. Therefore, information about public services and goods, for example, should be available, as far as possible, also in languages spoken by minorities and States parties should ensure that any language requirements relating to employment and education are based on reasonable and objective criteria.[12]

Religion

As concerns religion, the Social Rights Committee holds,

> This prohibited ground of discrimination covers the profession of religion or belief of one's choice (including the non-profession of any religion or belief), that may be publicly or privately manifested in worship, observance, practice and teaching.[13] For instance, discrimination arises when persons belonging to a religious minority are denied equal access to universities, employment, or health services on the basis of their religion.[14]

Discrimination based on nationality

The Social Rights Committee's elaborations and explorations of this area are done with an explicit nod to the previous work of the CERD Committee. This Committee was compelled to examine the line between ban in discrimination based on ethnicity or perceived race on the one hand, and nationality on the other, as a result of provisions of the ICERD, which would potentially nullify the object and purpose of the treaty, in contravention of the Vienna Law on Treaties. Particularly at issue were Articles 1(2) and 1(3).[15]

The result of this probing of the line between discrimination based on perceived race or ethnicity on the one hand, and nationality on the other, is CERD General Comment 30 'Discrimination against Non-Citizens'. Space considerations preclude a comprehensive treatment of General Comment 30 here. However, of relevance are the ten paragraphs devoted explicitly to economic, social and cultural rights, setting out that the States parties to the Convention, 'as appropriate to their specific circumstances', adopt the following measures:

1 Remove obstacles that prevent the enjoyment of economic, social and cultural rights by non-citizens, notably in the areas of education, housing, employment and health;
2 Ensure that public educational institutions are open to non-citizens and children of undocumented immigrants residing in the territory of a State party;
3 Avoid segregated schooling and different standards of treatment being applied to non-citizens on the grounds of race, colour, descent and national or ethnic origin in elementary and secondary school and with respect to access to higher education;
4 Guarantee the equal enjoyment of the right to adequate housing for citizens and non-citizens, especially by avoiding segregation in housing, and ensuring that housing agencies refrain from engaging in discriminatory practices;
5 Take measures to eliminate discrimination against non-citizens in relation to working conditions and work requirements, including employment rules and practices with discriminatory purposes or effects;
6 Take effective measures to prevent and redress the serious problems commonly faced by non-citizen workers, in particular by non-citizen domestic workers, including debt bondage, passport retention, illegal confinement, rape and physical assault;
7 Recognize that, while States parties may refuse to offer jobs to non-citizens without a work permit, all individuals are entitled to the enjoyment of labour and employment rights, including the freedom of assembly and association, once an employment relationship has been initiated until it is terminated;
8 Ensure that States parties respect the right of non-citizens to an adequate standard of physical and mental health by, inter alia, refraining

from denying or limiting their access to preventive, curative and palliative health services;

9 Take the necessary measures to prevent practices that deny non-citizens their cultural identity, such as legal or de facto requirements that non-citizens change their name in order to obtain citizenship and to take measures to enable non-citizens to preserve and develop their culture; and

10 Ensure the right of non-citizens, without discrimination based on race, colour, descent and national or ethnic origin, to have access to any place or service intended for use by the general public, such as transport, hotels, restaurants, cafés, theatres and parks.[16]

While CERD General Comment 30 has been criticized for, in some areas, representing a narrow interpretation of the scope of the rights at issue, the CERD Committee was fairly exhaustive in its digestion of relevant national and international jurisprudence as concerns non-citizens, at least as of the year 2004, when General Comment 30 was adopted.[17] Of note also are the particular categories of persons of concern named by the CERD Committee: 'non-citizens', 'non-citizen workers', 'non-citizen domestic workers' and 'children of undocumented immigrants'.

Finally, the wording of the raw text of certain treaties makes it evident that certain rights are extended to all people unequivocally, without any form of proportionality or other test. For example, Article 28 of the Child Rights Convention sets out that primary education shall be 'compulsory and available free to *all*', as well as that secondary education shall be 'available and accessible to *every child*'. Under the same treaty provision, 'educational and vocational information and guidance available and accessible to *all children*' (emphases added).

Conclusions

The words of the Universal Declaration exhort States to action on behalf of the stranger in our midst and that 'every individual and every organ of society' shall strive 'to promote respect for these rights and freedoms . . . to secure their universal and effective recognition and observance.' In law, these commitments play out in a range of ways, including as follows:

1 The international human rights treaties guarantee rights to 'everyone', without regard to citizenship, in keeping with our global commitment that all persons are born equal in dignity and in rights. In the area of economic, social and cultural rights, as per authoritative interpretation, Article 2(2) of the Social Rights Covenant obliges each State

Party to guarantee the rights enunciated in the Covenant regardless of nationality;

2   The relevant UN human rights bodies – as well as national and supranational adjudicating bodies – have increasingly provided details as to the scope and content of various economic, social and cultural rights, such as in the core areas of education, employment and work; health, social security and social assistance; and child and family protection – a non-exhaustive list; and

3   Certain economic, social and cultural rights, such as the right to primary education for all children, are absolute in quality.

Notes

1   This book does not use the term 'integration' due to the rather menacing connotations that term has taken on in the past decade, frequently associated with very stringent requirements of language competence and cultural trivia awareness, at odds with the requirements of equal dignity set out under international human rights law.

2   A/71/L.1, para 3.

3   See mutatis mutandis CESCR Committee General Comment 3 on the nature of States' Parties obligations.

4   See, for example, General Comment 15 on the right to water or General Comment 19 on the right to social security.

5   E/C.12/GC/20, para 5.

6   Ibid. para 24.

7   Ibid. para 30. The Human Rights Committee has similarly interpreted "other status" to include "nationality" (Communication No. 196/1985, Gueye et al v. France. Views adopted by the Human Rights Committee on para 9.4.).

8   Ibid.

9   Ibid. para 26.

10 Outcome Document Durban Review Conference, paragraph 6: 'Reaffirms that all peoples and individuals constitute one human family, rich in diversity, and that all human beings are born free and equal in dignity and rights; and strongly rejects any doctrine of racial superiority along with theories which attempt to determine the existence of so-called distinct human races'.

11 E/C.12/GC/20, para 19.

12 Ibid. para 21.

13 See also General Assembly's Declaration on the Elimination of All Forms of Intolerance and of Discrimination Based on Religion or Belief, proclaimed by General Assembly resolution 36/55 of 25 November 1981.

14 E/C.12/GC/20, para 22.

15 ICERD Article 1 states,

> 1   In this Convention, the term 'racial discrimination' shall mean any distinction, exclusion, restriction or preference based on race, colour, descent, or national or ethnic origin which has the purpose or effect of nullifying or impairing the recognition, enjoyment or exercise, on an equal footing, of human rights and fundamental freedoms in the political, economic, social, cultural or any other field of public life.

2   This Convention shall not apply to distinctions, exclusions, restrictions or preferences made by a State Party to this Convention between citizens and non-citizens.

3   Nothing in this Convention may be interpreted as affecting in any way the legal provisions of States Parties concerning nationality, citizenship or naturalization, provided that such provisions do not discriminate against any particular nationality.

16   CERD/C/64/Misc.11/rev.3, paras. 29–38.

17   Including for example CERD's own jurisprudence on discrimination against non-citizens (CERD Yilmaz v Netherlands 10 August 1988, CERD/C/36/D/1/1984 and CERD May 2016, Gabaroum v France, CERD/C/89/D52/2012), as well as European Court of Human Rights jurisprudence pursuant to the case of Gaygusuz v. Austria in which the Court ruled that Austria had violated the European Convention on Human Rights Article 14 ban on discrimination by denying Turkish workers in Austria unemployment insurance.

8   Rights at work

Bjarney Friðriksdóttir

A migrant woman was employed for more than two years in the Netherlands when she was injured at work and had to take sick leave. She returned to work part time the following year but the employer terminated her contract when at that time she was pregnant. The employer confirmed that a national worker would have been treated differently.

Yilmaz – Dogan v The Netherlands, Committee on the Elimination of Racial Discrimination violation of ICERD Communication No. 1/1984, UN Doc. CERD/C/36/D/1/1984 (1988).

> We will pay particular attention to the application of minimum labour standards for migrant workers regardless of their status, as well as to recruitment and other migration-related costs, remittance flows, transfers of skills and knowledge and the creation of employment opportunities for young people.
> New York Declaration of the UN General Assembly
> 19 September 2016[1]

Standards on rights at work are set out in international human rights law and most extensively in international labour law. The Universal Declaration provides for some key rights at work such as that everyone has the right to work, to free choice of employment and just and favourable conditions of work, the right to equal pay for equal work without discrimination, to just and favourable remuneration for their work, to form and join trade unions[2] and the right to rest and leisure, including reasonable limitations of working hours.[3] These rights should be guaranteed to everyone regardless of nationality in accordance with the principle of equal treatment set forth in the Universal Declaration, which recognizes that all human beings are born free and equal in dignity and rights,[4] that everyone is entitled to all the rights enshrined therein without distinction of any kind[5] and that all persons are equal before the law and are entitled without any discrimination to equal protection of the law.[6]

This fundamental principle of equality before the law and entitlement to the equal protection of the law without any discrimination[7] is also enshrined in the Civil and Political Rights Covenant and is in itself an autonomous right, while it 'prohibits discrimination in law or in fact in any field regulated and protected by public authorities.' It is a substantive right that imposes an obligation 'on State parties in regard to their legislation and the application thereof,' that the content of legislation 'should not be discriminatory.'[8] This fundamental principle is applicable to all rights at work set forth in national legislation and international instruments addressing rights at work.

International human rights law

The Social Rights Covenant recognizes the 'right of everyone' to, among other rights, the right to work, which includes the right to the opportunity to gain a living by work freely chosen or accepted, the enjoyment of just and favourable conditions of work, to form trade unions and join a trade union of one's own choice and the right to social security, including social insurance. The personal scope of the Covenant 'applies to everyone including migrants, such as refugees, asylum-seekers, stateless persons, migrant workers and victims of international trafficking, regardless of legal status and documentation.'[9] The right to work[10] in the Covenant is interpreted as a 'general and non-exhaustive' right which includes the right of everyone to the opportunity to gain his or her living by work which he or she freely chooses or accepts.[11] In regard to the principle of non-discrimination as it relates to migrants, the right to work 'should apply in relation to employment opportunities for migrant workers and their families.'[12]

The right to fair wages and adequate working conditions[13] addresses, among other factors, the right to fair wages and equal remuneration for work of equal value without distinction of any kind, safe and healthy working conditions and rest, leisure and reasonable limitations of working hours. These rights apply to 'all workers in all settings,' including workers in the informal sector, migrant workers, workers from ethnic and other minorities, domestic workers and refugee workers.[14] Whereas migrant workers, in particular if their status is irregular, are vulnerable to exploitation, long working hours, unfair wages and dangerous and unhealthy working environments, States parties to the Covenant should guarantee that laws and policies ensure that migrant workers enjoy treatment that is no less favourable than that of national workers in relation to remuneration and conditions of work.[15] Refugee workers, because of their often precarious status, remain vulnerable to exploitation, discrimination and abuse in the workplace. They may be less well paid than nationals and have longer working hours and more dangerous working conditions, which requires States parties to enact legislation enabling refugees to work and under conditions no less favourable than for nationals.[16] As regards domestic workers, the vast majority of whom are women and many of whom are migrants, they have the right to just and favourable conditions of work, including decent working conditions, paid annual leave, normal working hours, daily and weekly rest on the basis of equality with other workers, remuneration established without discrimination based on sex and social security.[17]

To ensure that all individuals can access adequate social security, States parties to the Covenant have an obligation to remove de facto discrimination on prohibited grounds and should 'ensure that legislation, policies, programmes and the allocation of resources facilitate access to social security for all members of society.'[18] In order to achieve this, they 'should give special attention to those individuals and groups who traditionally face difficulties in exercising this right,' including the unemployed, workers inadequately protected by social security, persons working in the informal economy, refugees, asylum seekers, internally displaced persons, returnees and migrants.[19] Migrants, including migrant workers who have 'contributed to a social security scheme, should be able to benefit from that contribution or retrieve their contribution if they leave the country.'[20] These rights should be guaranteed in accordance with the principle of equal protection of the law discussed earlier.[21] Migrants should also be able to access non-contributory schemes for income support, affordable access to health care and family support. Any restrictions, 'including a qualification period, must be proportionate and reasonable,' and all persons, 'irrespective of their nationality, residency or immigration status, are entitled to primary and emergency medical care.'[22]

In Article 5(e) ICERD, States have undertaken to prohibit and to eliminate racial discrimination in the enjoyment of the right to work, to free choice of employment, to just and favourable conditions of work, to protection against unemployment, to equal pay for equal work, to just and favourable remuneration and to the right to form and join trade unions.

The majority of the rights set forth in the Migrant Workers Convention are analogous to rights enshrined in the Social Rights Covenant and Civil and Political Rights Covenant. In the preamble to the Migrant Workers Convention, it is noted that migrant workers and their families frequently find themselves in a vulnerable situation due, among other factors, to 'the difficulties they may encounter arising from their presence in the State of employment.'[23] That there is a 'need to bring about the international protection of the rights of all migrant workers and members of their families, reaffirming and establishing basic norms in a comprehensive convention which could be applied universally.'[24] The Migrant Workers Convention addresses all migrant workers; the definition of its personal scope stipulates that it is applicable, except as otherwise provided, to all migrant workers and members of their families without distinction of any kind such as sex, race, colour, language, religion or conviction; political or other opinion; national, ethnic or social origin; nationality; age; economic position; property; marital status; birth; or other status.[25] Within the Convention, a distinction is made between regular and irregular migrants, but its core sections that provide for the rights of migrant workers are two, part III, which applies to all migrant workers and members of their families and part IV, which provides for other rights of migrant workers and members of their families who are documented or in a regular situation. Unlike general human rights instruments, the Migrant Workers Convention 'explicitly includes nationality among the prohibited grounds of discrimination,' and whereas the rights in part III of the Convention apply to all migrant workers and members of their families, including those in an irregular situation, any differential treatment based on nationality or migration status is considered to amount to discrimination unless the reasons for such differentiation are prescribed by law, pursue a legitimate aim under the Convention, are necessary in the specific circumstances, and proportionate to the legitimate aim pursued.[26]

International labour law

International labour law covers a wide spectrum of rights related to employment and social conditions, and the International Labour Organization (ILO) has repeatedly confirmed that 'all international labour standards apply to migrant workers, unless otherwise stated.' Furthermore, that the 'human rights of all migrant workers, regardless of their status, should be promoted and protected.' In particular, all migrant workers should benefit from the principles and rights in the 1998 ILO Declaration on Fundamental Principles and Rights at Work and its follow-up, which are reflected in the eight fundamental ILO Conventions[27] and the relevant UN human rights Conventions.[28]

ILO Migrant Workers Convention of 1949

Two ILO Conventions particularly address migrant workers. Those are Convention No. 97, Migration for Employment, and Convention No. 143, Migrant Workers. The personal scope of Convention No. 97 is limited to migrants regularly admitted for employment, and the term 'migrant for employment' includes a person who migrates between States for employment purposes and who is regularly admitted as a migrant for employment.[29] The central provision of the Convention in terms of protection of the rights of migrants addresses non-discrimination and provides that States parties undertake to apply treatment no less favourable than that which they apply to their own nationals in respect to remuneration, including family allowances, hours of work, holidays and pay, minimum age for employment, women's work and work of young persons, membership of trade unions and enjoyment of the benefits of collective bargaining and accommodation without discrimination in respect to nationality, race, religion or sex to immigrants lawfully within its territory. Furthermore, the non-discrimination clause applies to social security, including employment injury, maternity, sickness, invalidity, old age, death, unemployment, employment taxes and legal proceedings relating to the matters referred to in the Convention, however, only in so far as these are regulated by national law or regulations.[30] The equal treatment principle with respect to social security in the Convention 'applies to all migrant workers lawfully in the country, whether they have permanent or temporary residence status.'[31] Although 'the imposition of minimum requirements as regards the duration of residency or employment' in relation to non-contributory schemes 'would not necessarily be contrary to the Convention, if those conditions also apply to nationals,'[32] such arrangements 'do not permit the automatic exclusion of certain categories of workers from qualifying for social security benefits.'[33]

ILO Migrant Workers Convention of 1975

ILO Convention No. 143, Migrant Workers, which stipulates from the outset that it applies to all migrant workers, consists of two parts. Part I addresses migration in abusive conditions, and part II calls for equality of opportunity and treatment. Most of the provisions of part I aim at detecting and preventing irregular migration and the protection of migrants in irregular situations. In that respect, it provides that migrant workers, who have resided legally for the purpose of employment in the territory of a State, shall not be regarded as in an illegal or irregular situation solely due to loss of employment, which shall not in itself imply the withdrawal of authorization of residence or a work permit.[34] Furthermore, that a migrant shall enjoy equality of treatment with nationals in respect, in particular, to guarantees of security of employment, the provision of alternative employment, relief work and retraining.[35] As regards migrants who have been engaged in work without authorization, it provides that in cases in which laws and regulations to control movements of migrants for employment have not been respected, and where the irregular position of migrants cannot be regularized, migrants shall enjoy equality of treatment for themselves and their families in respect to rights arising out of past employment as regards remuneration, social security and other benefits.[36] Thus

> migrant workers in an irregular situation are entitled to those social security rights and benefits which they have acquired by virtue of their

period of employment and by fulfilling the other qualifying conditions required in the case of migrants in a regular situation.[37]

The personal scope of part II of the Convention extends to migrant workers who migrate or have migrated from one country to another with a view to being employed otherwise than on their own account and includes any person regularly admitted as a migrant worker. It calls for the adoption of a national policy to promote and guarantee equality of opportunity and treatment in respect to employment and occupation, including access to employment,[38] social security, trade union and cultural rights and individual and collective freedoms for persons who as migrant workers or as members of their families are lawfully within its territory. In addition, States parties are required to guarantee equality of treatment pertaining to working conditions for all migrant workers who perform the same activity, whatever might be the particular conditions of their employment.[39]

Domestic workers

In a general assessment on the personal scope of Conventions No. 97 and No. 143, the ILO Committee of Experts provided that the 'instruments do not distinguish between workers who migrate for permanent settlement, and those who migrate for short-term or seasonal work and who do not expect to stay for any significant length of time in the host country.' That other than for certain provisions that apply explicitly only to permanent migrant workers, 'no exemptions are envisaged in relation to any category of regular-entry migrant worker.'[40] ILO Convention No. 189, concerning decent work for domestic workers, reiterates that both of the Conventions listed earlier are of special relevance to domestic workers while many of them are migrants, but Convention No. 189 is set forth to recognize the special conditions under which domestic work is carried out, which makes it desirable to supplement general ILO standards with standards specific to domestic workers so as to enable them to enjoy their rights fully.[41] Convention No. 189 recalls several of the fundamental rights at work and requires States parties to take measures to respect, promote and realize these fundamental principles and rights at work.[42] It provides that national laws and regulations shall require that migrant domestic workers who are recruited in one country for domestic work in another receive a written job offer or contract of employment that is enforceable in the country in which the work is to be performed.[43] Furthermore, the Convention stipulates that each State party shall take measures towards ensuring equal treatment of domestic workers and workers generally in relation to normal hours of work, overtime compensation, periods of daily and weekly rest and paid annual leave,[44] and requires each State party to ensure that domestic workers enjoy minimum wage coverage, where such coverage exists, and that remuneration is established without discrimination based on sex.[45] The right of each domestic worker to a enjoy safe and healthy working environment is reiterated and States parties are required to take effective measures to ensure the occupational safety and health of domestic workers.[46] The duty of each State party to ensure that domestic workers enjoy conditions that are not less favourable than those applied to workers generally in respect of social security protection, including with respect to maternity that is provided for,[47] and measures that States party to it shall take to effectively protect domestic workers, including migrant domestic workers, recruited or placed by private employment agencies, against abusive practices are set forth.[48]

Conclusion

The analysis of international labour law in conjunction with international human rights law revels the following:

1   Rights at work apply to lawfully resident migrant workers, and their equal treatment with nationals must be ensured irrespective of their length of stay as migrant workers, their nationality and the type of work they are engaged in;
2   Irregularly resident workers are entitled to protection of their rights at work and other fundamental rights regardless of their status; and
3   The prohibition of discrimination based on nationality applies to migrant workers, and they must be granted equality before the law and equal protection of the law at the national level in the State where they reside and work.

Notes

1   A/71/L.1 para 57.
2   Universal Declaration Article 23.
3   Universal Declaration Article 24.
4   Universal Declaration Article 1.
5   Universal Declaration Article 2.
6   Universal Declaration Article 7.
7   Civil and Political Rights Covenant Article 26.
8   Human Rights Committee, General Comment No. 18, Non-discrimination (1989), paragraph 12.
9   Committee on Economic, Social and Cultural Rights, General Comment No. 20, Non-discrimination in Economic, Social and Cultural Rights (2009), para 30
10 Social Rights Covenant Article 6.

11 Social Rights Committee, General Comment No.18, The Right to Work (Art, 6), (2005), para 2.
12 Ibid. para 18.
13 Social Rights Covenant Article 7.
14 Social Rights Committee, General Comment No. 23, On the Right to Just and Favourable Conditions of Work (Article 7), (2016), para 5.
15 Ibid. para 47(e).
16 Ibid. para 47(i).
17 Ibid. para 47(f).
18 Social Rights Committee, General Comment No.19, The Right to Social Security (Art, 9), (2008), para 30.
19 Ibid. para 31.
20 Ibid. para 36.
21 See for example Gueye v. France, available at http://hrlibrary.umn.edu/undocs/session35/196-1985.html
22 Social Rights Committee, General Comment No.19, The Right to Social Security (Art, 9), (2008), para 37.
23 Preamble of Migrant Workers Convention, recital 9.
24 Preamble of Migrant Workers Convention, recital 15.
25 Migrant Workers Convention Article 1(1).
26 Migrant Workers Committee General Comment No. 2 on the rights of migrant workers in an irregular situation and members of their families (2013), para 18.
27 These are Freedom of Association and Protection of the Right to Organize Convention, 1948 (No. 87) and Right to Organize and Collective Bargaining Convention, 1949 (No. 98); Forced Labour Convention, 1930 (No. 29) and Abolition of Forced Labour Convention, 1957 (No. 105); Equal Remuneration Convention, 1951 (No. 100); Discrimination (Employment and Occupation) Convention, 1958 (No. 111); Minimum Wage Convention, 1973 (No. 138); Worst Forms of Child Labour Convention, 1999 (No. 182).
28 ILO Multilateral Framework on Labour Migration: Non-binding principles and guidelines for a rights-based approach to labour migration. 2006. Geneva, International Labour Office, paragraph 9(a) and 8.
29 Article 11(1) ILO Convention No. 97.
30 Article 6(1) ILO Convention No. 97.
31 International Labour Conference, 105th Session 2016, Promoting Fair Migration, Report of the Committee of Experts on the Application of Covenants and Recommendations (articles 19, 22 and 35 of the Constitution), Report III (Part 1 B). Geneva: International Labour Office, 389.
32 Ibid. 390.
33 Ibid. 391.
34 Article 8(1) ILO Convention No. 143.
35 Article 8(2) ILO Convention No. 143.
36 Article 9(1) ILO Convention No. 143.
37 International Labour Conference, 105th Session 2016, Promoting Fair Migration, Report of the Committee of Experts on the Application of Covenants and Recommendations (articles 19, 22 and 35 of the Constitution), Report III (Part 1 B). Geneva: International Labour Office, 314.
38 Article 10 ILO Convention No. 143. (Note that Article 14 permits limiting free choice of employment for a period up to two years.)
39 Article 12(g) ILO Convention No. 143.

40 International Labour Conference, 105th Session 2016, Promoting Fair Migration, Report of the Committee of Experts on the Application of Covenants and Recommendations (articles 19, 22 and 35 of the Constitution), Report III (Part 1 B). Geneva: International Labour Office, 111.
41 ILO Convention No. 189, paras 7 and 8 of preamble.
42 Article 3 ILO Convention No. 189.
43 Article 8(1) ILO Convention No. 189.
44 Article 10 ILO Convention No. 189.
45 Article 11 ILO Convention No. 189.
46 Article 13 ILO Convention No. 189.
47 Article 14 ILO Convention No. 189.
48 Article 1 ILO Convention No. 189.

9 Family life and the migrant

Rowena Moffatt, Ella Gunn and Anuscheh Farahat

A migrant who was a refugee in a host state sought family reunification with his spouse and three children who remained in the home state. The home state refused to allow them to leave because of the migrant's political views.

Human Rights Committee El Dernawi & Ors v Libyan Arab Jamahiriya Communication No 1143/2002 UN Doc CCPR/C/90/D/1143/2002 (2007) violation of the Civil and Political Rights Covenant 20 July 2007.

> We will consider facilitating opportunities for safe, orderly and regular migration, including, as appropriate, employment creation, labour mobility at all skills levels, circular migration, family reunification and education-related opportunities.
>
> New York Declaration of the UN General Assembly
> 19 September 2016[1]

The Universal Declaration was the first document to pronounce the importance of the family unit as a concept deserving protection at international law. Article 16(3) of the Universal Declaration provides that 'the family is the natural and fundamental group unit of society and is entitled to protection by society and the State'.[2] The Human Rights Committee has given an inclusive and pluralistic definition of 'family'. In its General Comments, the Human Rights Committee has stated that 'family' be given 'a broad interpretation to include all those comprising the family as understood in the society of the State party concerned',[3] noting that the concept of 'family' may differ between States, or region to region within a State. Although this may mean it is not possible to formulate a universal definition of 'family', when a group of individuals are regarded as a family under legislation and the practice of the relevant State, that family life is entitled to protection.[4] The existence or non-existence of family life is a question of fact, depending on the existence in practice, of close personal ties in accordance with respective domestic regulations. Whilst the fundamental importance of the family is recognised in international standards, and migrants are entitled to the protection of this right, they do not have an unqualified right to choose the country in which to enjoy family life, and a State may, in certain circumstances, interfere with the right, provided the interference is proportionate and not arbitrary. This will inevitably be a fact-specific enquiry that often requires a balancing of individual interests against State interests.

Prohibition on and protection against arbitrary interference

Article 12 of the Universal Declaration and Article 17 of the Civil and Political Rights Covenant prohibit arbitrary interference with 'privacy, family, home or correspondence' and provide that everyone has the right to the protection of the law against such interferences. Article 17 extends the prohibition to include 'unlawful interferences'. The Human Rights Committee views the phrase 'arbitrary interference' as encompassing interferences provided for under the law and notes that even where interferences are provided for in this manner, they should nevertheless be reasonable in the circumstances.[5]

The Human Rights Committee has made clear that the terms of the Civil and Political Rights Covenant 'must be guaranteed without discrimination between citizens and aliens', and, in particular, that aliens must not be subjected to arbitrary or unlawful interference with their rights to family life.[6] This prohibition and associated protection has been specifically recognised in the context of establishing those rights which should be afforded to migrant workers and their families in the form of Article 14 of the Migrant Workers Convention.[7]

Requirement of affirmative action to protect – family reunification

In addition to the protections that are to be afforded by the law, both Covenants establish a requirement on the part of the State to engage in *affirmative action* to ensure family units are protected. Article 10(1) of the Social Rights Covenant states that 'the widest possible protection and assistance' should be afforded to a family, in particular for its establishment, and Article 23(1) of the Civil and Political Rights Covenant mandates that family units are 'entitled to protection by society and the State'.

These rights are further expanded upon as they relate to children. The Social Rights Covenant at Article 10(3) requires that 'special measures of protection and assistance should be taken on behalf of all children and young persons without any discrimination for reasons of parentage or other conditions', while Article 24(1) of the Civil and Political Rights Covenant states that every child is to have, without discrimination, 'the right to such measures of protection as are required by his status as a minor, on the part of his family, society and the State'.[8]

The requirement of affirmative action was later recognised in 1975 by the International Labour Organisation. In its Migrant Workers Recommendation (No. 151), the ILO made clear that countries of employment and countries of origin should use 'all possible measures' to facilitate the reunification of families of migrant workers, including by ensuring that a migrant worker has appropriate accommodation which meets the standards normally applicable to nationals of the country of employment.[9] In order to facilitate this reunification, the ILO recommended that States take into account the needs of migrant workers and their families when developing their own domestic policies as to the development of and access to housing and reception services.[10]

The Human Rights Committee has explicitly recognised the relevance of Article 23 to the reunification of families. For example, in the case of *Ngambi and Nebol v France*,[11] it stated that Article 23

> guarantees the protection of family life including the interest in family reunification. . . . The protection of such family is not necessarily obviated, in any particular case, by the absence of formal marriage bonds, especially where there is a local practice of customary or common law marriage. Nor is the right to protection of family life necessarily displaced by geographical separation, infidelity, or the absence of conjugal relations.

Moreover, it is suggested that these articles, combined with the obligation provided under the Child Rights Convention to ensure that the best interests of the child is a primary consideration in decision making,[12] mean that decisions regarding child refugees or migrants must be affected in a way which ensures that the family unit remains intact. Likewise, the Human Rights Committee has expressed the view that administrative practices and migration control measures be 'compatible with the principles and standards of applicable refugee and human rights law'.[13]

Protection against removal

Decisions of the Human Rights Committee illustrate the significance of the protection of family life in the context of removal. In *Madafferi v Australia*, it was held that when deciding whether removal is justified, the State must weigh the significance of the reason for deportation with the hardship the family and its members are likely to face following removal.[14] In *Farag El Dernawi v Libyan Arab Jamahiriya*, the Human Rights Committee noted that where a State party cannot provide a justification for interfering with family life (for example, as in this case, by stripping citizens of their passport and therefore preventing family reunion), such interference will be arbitrary, in violation of Article 17.[15]

Rights to marry and found a family

Article 16(1) of the Universal Declaration and Article 23(2) of the Civil and Political Rights Covenant establish the right of men and women to marry and found a family. A requirement that both spouses must freely consent to marriage is also provided by Article 16(2) of the Universal Declaration, Article 10 of the 'Economic Rights Covenant' and Article 23(3) of the Civil and Political Rights Covenant. Both Article 16(1) of the Universal Declaration and Article 23(4) of the Civil and Political Rights Covenant mandate that spouses in a marriage are to have equal rights during the marriage and upon its dissolution. All of these rights are recognised by Article 16 of CEDAW.

The Human Rights Committee has stated that this right to found a family indicates a 'possibility to procreate and live together', which implies the adoption of measures domestically and sometimes in cooperation with other States to ensure that families are united or reunited, particularly in circumstances where family members become separated for political or economic reasons.[16]

Conclusion

International law regards the family as the fundamental unit within society, and a number of significant rights flow from this status. The following rights are to be afforded to individuals and are to be implemented without discrimination between citizens and aliens:

1   Family life is not to be arbitrarily or unlawfully interfered with;
2   The law of a State must operate to protect against such interferences;
3   States are to engage in affirmative action to ensure family units are protected and are to adopt special measures for the protection of children;
4   Men and women have the right to marry and establish a family;
5   Marriage is to be entered into with the free consent of both spouses; and
6   Equal rights are to be afforded to both spouses in a marriage.

Notes

1 A/71/L.1 para 57.
2 This statement was later reprised in Civil and Political Rights Covenant Article 23(1) and the Social Rights Covenant Article 10(1).
3 Human Rights Committee, General Comment No. 16: Article 17 (Right to Privacy), The Right to Respect of Privacy, Family, Home and Correspondence, and Protection of Honour and Reputation, 8 April 1988, para [5]. The General Comment is made in the context of Article 17 Civil and Political Rights Covenant.
4 Human Rights Committee, General Comment No. 19: Article 23 (The Family) Protection of the Family, the Right to Marriage and Equality of the Spouses, 27 July 1990.
5 Human Rights Committee General Comment No. 16: Article 17 (Right to Privacy), The Right to Respect of Privacy, Family, Home and Correspondence, and Protection of Honour and Reputation, 8 April 1988, available at www.refworld.org/docid/453883f922.html [accessed 2 March 2017], para 4.
6 Human Rights Committee General Comment No. 15: The Position of Aliens under the Covenant, 11 April 1986, available at www.refworld.org/docid/45139acfc.html [accessed 2 March 2017], paras 2, 7.
7 See also Human Rights Committee in Concluding Observations: Switzerland, 8 November 1996, CCPR/C/79/Add.70 noting that Swiss provisions that permitted family reunification for migrant workers only after 18 months was 'too long a period for the foreign worker to be separated from his family', para 18.
8 See also Child Rights Convention Article 3(1) requiring the best interests of children to be a primary consideration in actions concerning children.
9 www.ilo.org/dyn/normlex/en/f?p=NORMLEXPUB:12100:0::NO::P12100_ILO_CODE:R151, Article 13. www.ilo.org/dyn/normlex/en/f?p=NORMLEXPUB:12100:0::NO::P12100_ILO_CODE:R151, Article 13.
10 www.ilo.org/dyn/normlex/en/f?p=NORMLEXPUB:12100:0::NO::P12100_ILO_CODE:R151, Article 16.
11 Human Rights Committee Communication No 1179/2003, UN Doc. CCPR/C/81/D/1179/2003.
12 Child Rights Convention Article 3(1).
13 UNHCR Executive Committee Conclusion No 85 – Conclusion on international protection 1999, available at www.unhcr.org/uk/excom/exconc/3ae68c6e30/conclusion-international-protection.html
14 Human Rights Committee Francesco Madafferi v. Australia, Communication No. 1011/2001, U.N. Doc. CCPR/C/81/D/1011/2001 (2004), [9.8]
15 Human Rights Committee El Dernawi v Libyan Arab Jamahiriya Communication No 1143/2002 U.N. Doc CCPR/C/90/D/1143/2002 (2007).
16 Human Rights Committee, General Comment No. 19: Article 23 (The Family) Protection of the Family, the Right to Marriage and Equality of the Spouses, 27 July 1990, available at www.refworld.org/docid/45139bd74.html, [5].

10 Freedom of thought, belief and religion and freedom of expression and opinion

Susie Alegre

The State party should ensure the real and effective implementation of the right to peaceful assembly and freedom of association for all migrant workers, without the exercise of these rights becoming grounds for loss of employment or for the deportation of the persons involved.

Concluding observations of the Human Rights Committee Dominican Republic 12–30 March 2012.

> Gathered today at the United Nations, the birthplace and custodian of these universal values, we deplore all manifestations of xenophobia, racial discrimination and intolerance. We will take a range of steps to counter such attitudes and behaviour, in particular with regard to hate crimes, hate speech and racial violence.
>
> New York Declaration of the UN General Assembly 19 September 2016[1]

Freedom of thought, belief and religion along with freedom of expression and opinion are protected under both the Universal Declaration and the Civil and Political Rights Covenant in their Articles 18 and 19. Everyone is entitled to these rights and freedoms without distinction of any kind, such as race, colour, sex, language, religion, political or other opinion, national or social origin, property, birth or other status.[2] The obligation to respect these freedoms is binding on every State party as a whole whatever branch or level of the State is involved. States also have an obligation to ensure people are protected from acts by private persons or entities that might interfere with their enjoyment of these freedoms.[3]

Freedom of thought, belief and religion

Article 18 Civil and Political Rights Covenant states the following:

1   Everyone shall have the right to freedom of thought, conscience and religion. This right shall include freedom to have or to adopt a religion or belief of his choice, and freedom, either individually or in community with others and in public or private, to manifest his religion or belief in worship, observance, practice and teaching.

2   No one shall be subject to coercion which would impair his freedom to have or to adopt a religion or belief of his choice.

3   Freedom to manifest one's religion or beliefs may be subject only to such limitations as are prescribed by law and are necessary to protect public safety, order, health, or morals or the fundamental rights and freedoms of others.

4   The States Parties to the present Covenant undertake to have respect for the liberty of parents and, when applicable, legal guardians to ensure the religious and moral education of their children in conformity with their own convictions.

The Human Rights Committee clarified the scope and importance of freedom of thought, religion and belief in Article 18 Civil and Political Rights Covenant in its General Comment 22 of 1993:[4]

1   The Committee draws the attention of States parties to the fact that the freedom of thought and the freedom of conscience are protected equally with the freedom of religion and belief. The fundamental character of these freedoms is also reflected in the fact that this provision cannot be derogated from, even in time of public emergency, as stated in Article 4 (2) of the Covenant.

3   Article 18 distinguishes the freedom of thought, conscience, religion or belief from the freedom to manifest religion or belief. It does not permit any limitations whatsoever on the freedom of thought and conscience or on the freedom to have or adopt a religion or belief of one's choice. These freedoms are protected unconditionally, as is the right of everyone to hold opinions without interference in Article 19 (1). In accordance with Articles 18 (2) and 17, no one can be compelled to reveal his thoughts or adherence to a religion or belief.

In relation to migrants, the non-derogability of these freedoms is important. This means that no limitations can be justified, even in times of public emergency, and these freedoms must be respected for all irrespective of their immigration status. The prohibition on compelling someone to reveal their thoughts or adherence to a religion or belief is of particular importance in the context of migration, as it means that these factors cannot be taken into account in decisions on the status or rights of migrants. Actions such as requiring a person to provide access to information held on smartphones or computers could amount to a breach of this right insofar as they may force a person to reveal thoughts and beliefs they have not made public.[5] If the reason for this is to sanction them by, for example, refusing entry to a country, this would be a severe interference with their rights.

The freedom to manifest thought, belief or religion is not absolutely protected in the same way as the freedom to hold those thoughts, beliefs or religion. But despite that, it cannot be limited in a discriminatory way. The freedom extends to the educational sphere and may be of particular relevance for migrants in countries where their religion or belief structure is not the same as the majority:

6   The Committee notes that public education that includes instruction in a particular religion or belief is inconsistent with Article 18 (4) unless provision is made for non-discriminatory exemptions or alternatives that would accommodate the wishes of parents and guardians.[6]

Freedom of opinion and expression

Article 19 Civil and Political Rights Covenant states the following:

1   Everyone shall have the right to hold opinions without interference.
2   Everyone shall have the right to freedom of expression; this right shall include freedom to seek, receive and impart information and ideas of all kinds, regardless of frontiers, either orally, in writing or in print, in the form of art, or through any other media of his choice.
3   The exercise of the rights provided for in paragraph 2 of this Article carries with it special duties and responsibilities. It may therefore be subject to certain restrictions, but these shall only be such as are provided by law and are necessary:

   (a)   For respect of the rights or reputations of others;
   (b)   For the protection of national security or of public order (ordre public), or of public health or morals.

These freedoms are clearly linked to the freedom of thought, conscience and religion, and the Human Rights Committee has expanded on the freedom of opinion aspect of the right in its General Comment 34 of 2011:[7]

9   Paragraph 1 of Article 19 requires protection of the right to hold opinions without interference. This is a right to which the Covenant permits no exception or restriction. Freedom of opinion extends to the right to change an opinion whenever and for whatever reason a person so freely chooses. No person may be subject to the impairment of any rights under the Covenant on the basis

of his or her actual, perceived or supposed opinions. All forms of opinion are protected, including opinions of a political, scientific, historic, moral or religious nature. It is incompatible with paragraph 1 to criminalize the holding of an opinion. The harassment, intimidation or stigmatization of a person, including arrest, detention, trial or imprisonment for reasons of the opinions they may hold, constitutes a violation of Article 19, paragraph 1.

10   Any form of effort to coerce the holding or not holding of any opinion is prohibited. Freedom to express one's opinion necessarily includes freedom not to express one's opinion.

Freedom of opinion, therefore, means that migrants should not be discriminated against because of their opinions or their refusal to express their opinions.

In the modern world, freedom of expression operates across borders and the protections attach to a broad range of forms of expression which are increasingly important in light of the development of the Internet and social media as platforms for expression:

11   Paragraph 2 requires States parties to guarantee the right to freedom of expression, including the right to seek, receive and impart information and ideas of all kinds regardless of frontiers. This right includes the expression and receipt of communications of every form of idea and opinion capable of transmission to others, subject to the provisions in Article 19, paragraph 3, and Article 20. It includes political discourse, commentary on one's own and on public affairs, canvassing, discussion of human rights, journalism, cultural and artistic expression, teaching, and religious discourse. It may also include commercial advertising. The scope of paragraph 2 embraces even expression that may be regarded as deeply offensive, although such expression may be restricted in accordance with the provisions of Article 19, paragraph 3 and Article 20.[8]

Freedom of expression is fundamental to the protection of human rights and democracy. Some people may be at particular risk because of their activities in this sphere, and the Human Rights Committee highlighted the importance of protecting journalists, human rights defenders and others in this context. The requirement to protect such people from attack applies whether or not the individuals concerned are migrants:

23   States parties should put in place effective measures to protect against attacks aimed at silencing those exercising their right to freedom of expression. Paragraph 3 may never be invoked as a justification for the muzzling of any advocacy of multi-party democracy, democratic tenets and human rights. Nor, under any circumstance,

can an attack on a person, because of the exercise of his or her freedom of opinion or expression, including such forms of attack as arbitrary arrest, torture, threats to life and killing, be compatible with Article 19. Journalists are frequently subjected to such threats, intimidation and attacks because of their activities. So too are persons who engage in the gathering and analysis of information on the human rights situation and who publish human rights-related reports, including judges and lawyers. All such attacks should be vigorously investigated in a timely fashion, and the perpetrators prosecuted, and the victims, or, in the case of killings, their representatives, be in receipt of appropriate forms of redress.

Prohibition on discrimination and hate speech

ICERD makes clear that both hate speech and discrimination in the enjoyment of these rights is prohibited.[9] Freedom of expression may not be used as a platform for discrimination against migrants. In its General Comment 35[10] on Combating Racist Hate Speech, the CERD Committee stresses that States are under an obligation to

11   Take steps to address xenophobic attitudes and behaviour towards non-citizens, in particular hate speech and racial violence, and to promote a better understanding of the principle of non-discrimination in respect of the situation of non-citizens;

12   Take resolute action to counter any tendency to target, stigmatize, stereotype or profile, on the basis of race, colour, descent, and national or ethnic origin, members of 'non-citizen' population groups, especially by politicians, officials, educators and the media, on the Internet and other electronic communications networks and in society at large.

And the CERD Committee has also clarified, in its General Comment No. 30 (2005) on discrimination against non-citizens that States must

11   Take steps to address xenophobic attitudes and behaviour towards non-citizens, in particular hate speech and racial violence, and to promote a better understanding of the principle of non-discrimination in respect of the situation of non-citizens;

12   Take resolute action to counter any tendency to target, stigmatize, stereotype or profile, on the basis of race, colour, descent, and national or ethnic origin, members of "non-citizen" population groups, especially by politicians, officials, educators and the media, on the Internet and other electronic communications networks and in society at large.[11]

It is also important to stress that Article 18 may not be used as a basis for defending hate speech, which is clearly prohibited within the human rights framework:

> 7 According to Article 20, no manifestation of religions or beliefs may amount to propaganda for war or advocacy of national, racial or religious hatred that constitutes incitement to discrimination, hostility or violence. As stated by the Committee in its General Comment 11,[12] States parties are under the obligation to enact laws to prohibit such acts.[13]

Conclusions

The international human rights framework makes the following clear:

1 Discrimination based on religion, political or other opinion is unlawful.[14]
2 All people are entitled to equal protection against any discrimination in violation of international law and against any incitement to such discrimination.[15]
3 Discriminatory measures may be either direct or indirect in nature. This means that limitations on the rights of migrants that, while not explicitly referring to religion or political opinion, have a disproportionately adverse impact on people from a particular religion or political grouping, may be unlawful.

Notes

1 A/71/L.1 para 14.
2 Universal Declaration Article 2.
3 See for example Human Rights Committee General Comment 34 of 2011 on Article 19 CCPR/C/GC/34 para 7.
4 Human Rights Committee General Comment No 22 CCPR/C/GC/22.
5 See also www.researchgate.net/publication/261950057_Freedom_of_Thought_ in_the_Age_of_Neuroscience for discussion of implications for freedom of thought of sophisticated surveillance technologies that interpret outer evidence of inner states.
6 Human Rights Committee General Comment No 22 CCPR/C/GC/22.
7 Human Rights Committee General Comment No 34 CCPR/C/GC/34.
8 Human Rights Committee General Comment No 34 CCPR/C/GC/34.
9 ICERD Articles 4 and 5 (d)(vii)-(ix).
10 CERD Committee General Comment 35 /C/GC/35 of 26/09/2013.
11 CERD Committee General Comment 30 /C/GC/30.
12 Of 1983 on propaganda for war and inciting national, racial or religious hatred Human Rights Committee General Comment No 11 CCPR/C/GC/11.
13 Human Rights Committee General Comment No 22 CCPR/C/GC/22.
14 Universal Declaration Article 2.
15 Universal Declaration Article 7.

11 The right to an effective remedy, the right to an effective national procedure against arbitrary removal and the right to a fair hearing

Dana Baldinger

A migrant and asylum seeker sought international protection in a country. On national security grounds, the authorities there authorised his expulsion to the country where he feared persecution without a right of appeal with suspensive effect.

Agiza v. Sweden, Communication No. 233/2003, UN Doc. CAT/C/34/D/233/ 2003 (2005).

> Reaffirming that all individuals who have crossed or are seeking to cross international borders are entitled to due process in the assessment of their legal status, entry and stay, we will consider reviewing policies that criminalize cross- border movements.
>
> New York Declaration of the UN General Assembly
> 19 September 2016[1]

Rights without remedies have no power to assist people in disputes, particularly with state authorities. This chapter examines the international standards to remedies for migrants when the actions of states are challenged as incompatible with their human rights. Fair procedures and effective remedies are an indispensable part of international human rights law.

Effective national remedy: requirements under the Civil and Political Rights Covenant, Convention against Torture and Refugee Convention

Article 2(3) of the Civil and Political Rights Covenant accords a right to an effective remedy to any person who tenably asserts that a substantive Civil and Political Rights Covenant right has been violated. The Human

Rights Committee has made clear that Article (3) refers in the first place to judicial remedies.[2] It follows from General Comment No. 31(80) (2004) that, in order to be effective, the national remedy must be accessible and effective,[3] and that allegations of Covenant violations must be investigated promptly, thoroughly and effectively through independent and impartial bodies, which must be endowed with appropriate powers.[4]

Article 7 Civil and Political Rights Covenant also stipulates that no one shall be subjected to torture or to cruel, inhuman or degrading treatment or punishment. The Human Rights Committee has interpreted Article 7 in such a way that States parties must not expose individuals to the danger of torture or cruel, inhuman or degrading treatment or punishment upon return to another country by way of their extradition, removal or *refoulement*.[5] General Comment No. 20 stipulates that Article 7 should be read in conjunction with Article 2(3) and that Article 7 complaints must be investigated promptly and impartially by competent authorities so as to make the remedy effective.[6] In a number of cases concerning the torture and disappearance of individuals in dictatorial regimes, the Human Rights Committee has consistently ruled that Article 7, seen in conjunction with Article 2(3), requires from the national authorities, including national courts, that 'full investigations', or 'full and thorough inquiries',[7] are made. In a significant number of internal torture or disappearance cases, the Human Rights Committee found the inquiries made at national level non-compliant and concluded that there had been a violation of Article 2(3) in conjunction with Article 7.[8] In the case of *Pillai and Joachimpillai v. Canada* and the case of *X.H.L. v. the Netherlands* (both 2011), the Human Rights Committee deemed the national proceedings defective and therefore non-compliant with Article 7 because insufficient attention had been paid to statements on, respectively, past torture (Pillai) and the fate of ending up as a minor beggar in the street upon removal to China (X.H.L). In X.H.L., the Human Rights Committee concluded that there was a violation of Article 7 in conjunction with Article 24, the Civil and Political Rights Covenant provision on the best interest of the child.[9]

The Convention against Torture does not contain a separate provision on the right to an effective national remedy, but the Committee against Torture has derived this right from Article 3 of the Convention, the prohibition of *refoulement*. In the case of *Agiza v. Sweden* (2003),[10] the Committee against Torture stated,

> The Committee observes that the right to an effective remedy for a breach of the Convention underpins the entire Convention, for otherwise the protections afforded by the Convention would be rendered largely illusory. (. . .) The prohibition on *refoulement* contained in Article 3 should be interpreted (. . .) to encompass a remedy for its breach

(. . .). The nature of *refoulement* is such that an allegation of breach of that article relates to a future expulsion or removal; accordingly, the right to an effective remedy contained in Article 3 requires, in this context, an opportunity for effective, independent and impartial review of the decision to expel or remove, once that decision is made, when there is a plausible allegation that Article 3 issues arise.[11]

The Convention against Torture requires the possibility of appeal prior to removal. Sweden considered Agiza to be a serious threat to national security and decided to expel him to Egypt, his country of origin, for this reason. Agiza did not have an opportunity to lodge an appeal against this decision prior to his removal. According to the Committee, that practice constituted a violation of Article 3 in the Convention against Torture.[12]

National judicial proceedings cannot be qualified as Convention against Torture compliant – that is, effective, independent and impartial – if the evidence was evaluated in a clearly arbitrary way, if a denial of justice occurred or if the national officers clearly violated their obligations of impartiality.[13] There are a number of decisions in which the Committee against Torture reproached the national authorities for conducting insufficiently thorough investigations – for example, *A.S. v. Sweden* (2000)[14] and *Ke Chun Rong v. Australia* (2013).[15] In addition, in a number of decisions, the Committee against Torture has made clear that, in order to qualify as effective, judicial remedies must be more than a mere formality or reasonableness test and must make it possible to look at the substance (the merits) of the case. The first decision in which the Committee against Torture expressed this view was *Aung v. Canada* (2006).[16] The Committee against Torture considered that

> in the view of the Committee, the decisions of the Federal Court support the contention that applications for leave and judicial review are not mere formalities, but that the Federal Court may, in appropriate cases, look at the substance of a case.[17]

In the decision of *Nirmal Singh v. Canada* (2011),[18] the Committee against Torture concluded that the judicial review offered by the Federal Court of Canada did not constitute an effective national remedy. It articulated in a very clear way that States parties to the Convention against Torture are obliged to provide for judicial review of the merits, rather than merely of the reasonableness, of decisions on removal.[19]

The Refugee Convention does not contain a separate right to a national effective remedy. Article 16 of the Refugee Convention requires, however, that refugees have free access to the courts of law on the territory of all Contracting States. The majority of scholars assumes that Article 16 Refugee

Convention is applicable to contemporary judicial asylum proceedings.[20] On many occasions, the Human Rights Committee has expressed its opinion that national judges should be able to 'obtain a personal impression of the applicant' and that 'appeal or review proceedings should involve points of fact, including credibility, and points of law'.[21]

Effective national procedure against arbitrary removal: the requirement of equality of arms

Article 13 Civil and Political Rights Covenant provides to aliens protection against arbitrary removal. General Comment 15 (27) stipulates in paragraph 10 that

> An alien must be given full facilities for pursuing his remedy against removal so that this right will in all the circumstances of his case be an effective one. The principles of Article 13 relating to appeal against removal and the entitlement to review by a competent authority may only be departed from when 'compelling reasons of national security' so require.[22]

In the case of *Mansour Ahani v. Canada* (2004),[23] the Human Rights Committee concluded that there had been a violation of Article 13 because the national authorities breached the crucial requirements of equality of arms and adversarial proceedings. The national removal proceedings in *Ahani* were defective under Article 13, as the minister did not provide the author with all the materials – including secret information that Ahani was a danger to Canada's national security – on which the removal decision was based and the national courts did not correct this unfairness in the procedure.

The Committee against Torture has developed a similar approach in the case of *Sogi v. Canada* (2007).[24] The complainant in this case had applied for asylum in Canada. In August 2002, the Canadian Security and Intelligence Service issued a report stating that there were reasonable grounds to believe that the complainant was a member of the Babbar Khalsa International, classified as a terrorist group by Canadian law. A removal decision was taken as he was seen as a threat to Canada's national security. The information underpinning the national security rating was 'secret' and not disclosed to the complainant. The complainant applied for judicial review of the removal decision. The Federal Court concluded that the hearing officer had not erred in determining that certain information was relevant but could not be disclosed to the complainant for reasons of national security. The Federal Court considered it relevant that this secret information could, nevertheless, be taken into account by the Court itself so that a counterbalance was created. This ruling was upheld on appeal in a Federal Court of Appeal judgment.[25] The Committee against Torture ruled that the non-disclosure of this relevant evidence to the complainant resulted in a violation of the requirement of a fair hearing to persons subject to removal orders.[26] The decisions in *Mansour Ahani v. Canada* and *Sogi v. Canada* strongly convey the message that in removal cases, both parties to the case must have equal access to the documents in the case file.

Fair hearing by an impartial court

Article 14 Civil and Political Rights Covenant provides the right to a fair hearing by a competent, independent and impartial tribunal. The Human Rights Committee has, so far, been ambiguous about the question of whether or not this provision applies to national proceedings concerning migration and removal. In General Comment 32,[27] the Human Rights Committee explains the various requirements of Article 14. One of them is that courts and tribunals must hold fair hearings. The most important criterion of a fair hearing is the principle of equality of arms between the parties, which means that the same procedural rights are to be provided to all the parties. In addition, a fair hearing requires respect for the principle of adversarial proceedings, meaning that each party must be given the opportunity to contest all the arguments and evidence adduced by the other party.[28] A fair hearing also entails preclusion of *reformatio in pejus* (a claimant/plaintiff should not, as a result of a suit at law, end up worse off than before starting the proceedings) and expeditious procedure.[29]

In *Jansen-Gielen v. the Netherlands* (2001),[30] the Human Rights Committee concluded that there had been a violation of Article 14, first paragraph for reasons of non-compliance with the principles of equality of arms and adversarial proceedings. The highest national court in this case failed to take into account an expert report submitted by the author just a few days before the court hearing was scheduled to take place. The HRC found this incompatible with the principles of equality of arms and adversarial proceedings.

A fair hearing under Article 14 Civil and Political Rights Covenant must be offered by an independent and impartial tribunal established by law. According to General Comment 32, the requirement of impartiality has two aspects. First, judges must not allow their judgment to be influenced by personal bias or prejudice, nor harbour preconceptions about the particular case before them, nor act in ways that improperly promote the interests of one of the parties to the detriment of the other. Second, the tribunal must also appear to a reasonable observer to be impartial.

As set out earlier, the requirement of impartiality also forms part of Article 2(3) and Article 7 Civil and Political Rights Covenant and Article 3

Convention against Torture. In cases of allegations or suspicions of internal torture, the Committee against Torture has ruled that the requirement of impartiality obliges the national judge to make a meticulous reconstruction of what actually happened and to use investigative powers if that may help to come as close as possible to the truth.[31]

Conclusions: key features of national remedies and of a national court hearing

Migrants against whom a decision on removal is taken or to whom a residence permit has been denied have clear rights to an effective national remedy and a fair hearing by a national judge prior to removal or return to the country of origin. The UN treaties discussed earlier require the national court to perform a 'thorough and fair examination of the claim' (Human Rights Committee); an 'effective, independent and impartial review on the merits of the claim' (Committee against Torture); and 'appeal or review proceedings on points of fact, including credibility, and points of law' (Human Rights Committee).

Next, the conventions discussed earlier require the national judge to observe the important principle of equality of arms. In removal cases, both parties to the case must have equal access to the documents in the case file, including sensitive information on national security issues. Thus, the common denominator emerging from international law is independent, impartial, full and rigorous national judicial scrutiny, which guarantees equality of arms. This standard requires national courts to examine evidence in a careful and serious manner. It also requires that national courts are able to make an independent and fresh determination of the facts. If necessary in order to clarify the facts, national courts shall undertake judicial investigations such as hearing witnesses, ordering expert examinations and searching for additional information on the situation in countries of origin.

Notes

1 A/71/L.1 para 33.
2 See, for example, Human Rights Committee R.T. v. France, 30 March 1989, No. 162/87, para 7.4; Human Rights Committee José Vicente and others v. Colombia, 29 July 1997, No. 612/1995, para 5.2. See also Nowak 1993, p. 59, Boeles 1997, pp. 108–109, Nowak 2005, pp. 63–65.
3 Human Rights Committee General Comment No. 31(80) (2004).
4 Ibid. para.15.
5 Human Rights Committee, Kindler v. Canada, 18 November 1993, No. 470/1991.
6 Human Rights Committee General Comment No. 20: Replaces General Comment No. 7 concerning prohibition of torture and cruel treatment or punishment (Art. 7): 10/03/92, para 14.

84   *Dana Baldinger*

 7 Human Rights Committee, Irene Bleier Lewenhoff and Rosa Valino de Bleier v. Uruguay, 29 March 1982, No. 30/1978, para 11.1.
 8 See, for example, Human Rights Committee, Alberto Grille Motta v. Uruguay, 29 July 1980, No. 11/1977; Human Rights Committee, Delia Saldias de Lopez v. Uruguay, 29 July 1981, No. 52/1979; Human Rights Committee, Hugo Rodriguez v. Uruguay, 19 July 1994, No. 322/1988; Human Rights Committee, Bautista v. Colombia, 27 October 1995, No. 563/1993.
 9 Human Rights Committee Pillai and Joachimpillai v. Canada, 25 March 2011, No. 1763/2008, para 11.4, and X.H.L. v. the Netherlands, 2 September 2011, No. 1564/2007, paras. 10.1–10.7.
10 Committee against Torture, Agiza v. Sweden, 20 May 2005, No. 233/2003.
11 Ibid. paras. 13.6 and 13.7.
12 Ibid. paras 13.8.
13 See, for example, Committee against Torture, S.P.A. v. Canada, 7 November 2006, No. 282/2005, para 7.6.
14 Committee against Torture, A.S. v. Sweden, 24 November 2000, No. 149/1999.
15 Committee against Torture, Ke Chun Rong v. Australia, 7 February 2013, No. 416/2010.
16 Committee against Torture, Aung v. Canada, 15 May 2006, No. 273/2005.
17 Ibid. para 6.3.
18 Committee against Torture, Nirmal Singh v. Canada, 30 May 2011, No. 319/2007.
19 Ibid. paras. 8.8, 8.9, 9.
20 19 See, for example, Boeles 1997, pp. 71–77 Hathaway 2005, pp. 644–647.
21 See, for example, submission of the UNHCR in the Case of Mir Isfahani v. the Netherlands, Appl. No. 31252/03, May 2005, available at www.unhcr.org/refworld/docid/454f5e484.html [accessed 23 December 2012], paras. 31–42.
22 Human Rights Committee General Comment No. 15 (27) of 22 July 1986 on the rights of aliens.
23 Human Rights Committee, Mansour Ahani v. Canada, 15 June 2004, No. 1051/2002.
24 Committee against Torture Sogi v. Canada, 16 November 2007, No. 297/2006.
25 Ibid. paras. 2.1–2.11.
26 Ibid. paras. 10.4, 10.5.
27 Human Rights Committee General Comment No. 32 of 24 July 2007 'Equality before the courts and the right to a fair and public hearing by an independent court established by law'.
28 See, for example, Human Rights Committee, Jansen-Gielen v. the Netherlands, 3 April 2001, No. 846/1999, para 8.2.
29 In Human Rights Committee Morael v. France, 28 July 1989, No. 207/1986, these aspects of a fair hearing were mentioned for the first time; since then they have been repeated in many subsequent cases. See on expeditiousness General Comment No. 32, para 27.
30 Human Rights Committee, Jansen-Gielen v. the Netherlands, 14 May 2001, No. 846/1999.
31 For example Committee against Torture, M'Barek v. Tunisia, 10 November 1999, No. 060/1996.

12 Conclusion and summary of key international human rights of migrants

Elspeth Guild, Stefanie Grant and C. A. Groenendijk

> We reaffirm the purposes and principles of the Charter of the United Nations. We reaffirm also the Universal Declaration of Human Rights and recall the core international human rights treaties. We reaffirm and will fully protect the human rights of all refugees and migrants, regardless of status; all are rights holders. Our response will demonstrate full respect for international law and international human rights law and, where applicable, international refugee law and international humanitarian law.
>
> New York Declaration of the UN General Assembly
> 19 September 2016[1]

The New York Declaration reaffirms the UN member States' commitment to full protection of the human rights of migrants regardless of status. This solemn undertaking of all States in the UN General Assembly engages more than words – it reinforces the obligation which States already have in accordance with international human rights treaties and the Universal Declaration to take the necessary actions (and refrain from actions which are inconsistent) to uphold all human rights of migrants. This means not just those human rights which seem, to some State officials, unproblematic, but all human rights of migrants no matter whether they may seem complicated, politically sensitive or contrary to State policy, which itself is eternally ephemeral. Human rights are solid and have real consequences for State authorities and migrants. They are not simply political promises to the international community, they are obligations which are also instructions to all officials, including judges (and touching also the private sector and civil society), regarding how to carry out their tasks. If State border or migration authorities fail to conduct their activities in accordance with the State's international human rights obligations, then it will be up to the judges (and other complaints mechanisms) to hold them to those legal commitments and for lawyers to assist migrants in bringing their cases before a court of tribunal. Supranational remedies also exist and are very important, particularly as regards standard setting, but the heavy lifting of human rights compliance takes place at State borders and within their jurisdictions.

This book has examined the pressing issues which migrants encounter in their daily lives from the perspective of the correct application of international human rights obligations. It covers ten key situations where migrants and State authorities enter into contact and tension, and where migrants may need to be able to rely on their international human rights to obtain a just resolution. In these closing pages, we review the state of international human rights law as regards these ten subject areas and provide a short summary of the existing state of international law. All of these human rights are also upheld in the New York Declaration. So the purpose of this conclusion is to provide the reader (who may be short of time) with a checklist of human rights of migrants from which the Global Compact must build.

Right to legal personhood

> Everyone has the right to recognition as a person before the law.
> New York Declaration of the UN General Assembly
> 19 September 2016[2]

To ensure migrants are protected from 'civil death' and their rights are respected, States are required to acknowledge legal documentation from the country of origin of migrants, even if the administration in that country is far from reliable, or provide mechanisms for issuing documentation which enable migrants to prove who they are and legally to participate in the host society.

Rights at the border

> Recognizing that States have rights and responsibilities to manage and control their borders, we will implement border control procedures in conformity with applicable obligations under international law, including international human rights law and international refugee law.
> New York Declaration of the UN General Assembly
> 19 September 2016[3]

In order to comply with their obligations in international human rights law, States have a responsibility to adopt and implement border governance policies which are not discriminatory based on any prohibited grounds including nationality, race, colour, religion, political or other opinion, sex, gender identity, language, age or economic and social situation.

Immigration detention

> We will also pursue alternatives to detention while these assessments [admission, stay, removal] are under way.
>
> New York Declaration of the UN General Assembly
> 19 September 2016[4]

To protect the human rights of migrants, States must exhaustively enumerate in their legislation the permissible grounds, procedures and conditions for detention which comply with State obligations under international human rights law.

Irregular status

> We are committed to protecting the safety, dignity and human rights and fundamental freedoms of all migrants, regardless of their migratory status, at all times.
>
> New York Declaration of the UN General Assembly
> 19 September 2016[5]

To protect the human rights of migrants, States should establish procedures for regularly assessing, improving and monitoring the extent to which the human rights of all persons are equally enjoyed by migrants with irregular status.

Rights of residence, termination of residence and in respect of removal

> We will continue to protect the human rights and fundamental freedoms of all persons, in transit and after arrival.
>
> New York Declaration of the UN General Assembly
> 19 September 2016[6]

States have a duty to ensure the liberty of movement within the country to anyone lawfully residing, nationals or aliens, under the same conditions. If carrying out removal, States are obliged to strictly follow the procedure prescribed by law and evaluate all the individual circumstances that may impede it.

Economic, social and cultural rights of migrants and migrant inclusion

> We recall that our obligations under international law prohibit discrimination of any kind on the basis of race, colour, sex, language, religion,

political or other opinion, national or social origin, property, birth or other status.

New York Declaration of the UN General Assembly
19 September 2016[7]

States are under a duty to review policy, law and practice to ensure that the economic, social and cultural rights of all categories of migrants are respected, protected and fulfilled in line with States' commitments under international human rights law to secure the human rights set out under international treaty law to everyone.

Rights at work

We will pay particular attention to the application of minimum labour standards for migrant workers regardless of their status, as well as to recruitment and other migration-related costs, remittance flows, transfers of skills and knowledge and the creation of employment opportunities for young people.

New York Declaration of the UN General Assembly
19 September 2016[8]

Rights at work must be guaranteed to migrant workers on equal footing with national workers in accordance with the principle of non-discrimination, equality before the law and equal protection of the law.

Family life and the migrant

We will consider facilitating opportunities for safe, orderly and regular migration, including, as appropriate, employment creation, labour mobility at all skills levels, circular migration, family reunification and education-related opportunities.

New York Declaration of the UN General Assembly
19 September 2016[9]

States must pay due regard to the international legal principle that the family (however that concept is understood by the State concerned) is the fundamental group unit of society and therefore it is entitled to be protected. All of the rights flowing from that status need to be considered when States construct new laws and policies, and States should ensure that the rights apply equally to citizens and non-citizens without discrimination.

Freedom of thought, belief and religion and freedom of expression and opinion

Gathered today at the United Nations, the birthplace and custodian of these universal values, we deplore all manifestations of xenophobia, racial discrimination and intolerance. We will take a range of steps to counter such attitudes and behaviour, in particular with regard to hate crimes, hate speech and racial violence.

New York Declaration of the UN General Assembly
19 September 2016[10]

Migrants must not be obliged to reveal their thoughts, beliefs and opinions through, for example, examination of social media as part of an immigration process. Although migrants cannot be penalised for their thoughts, beliefs, religion or opinions, there is no such protection for hate speech. States are required to ensure that migrants are protected against discrimination based on their religion, belief or political opinions. This includes taking steps to prohibit hate speech against migrants.

The right to an effective remedy, the right to an effective national procedure against arbitrary removal and the right to a fair trial

Reaffirming that all individuals who have crossed or are seeking to cross international borders are entitled to due process in the assessment of their legal status, entry and stay, we will consider reviewing policies that criminalize cross- border movements.

New York Declaration of the UN General Assembly
19 September 2016[11]

In cases concerning removal or return of migrants, international human rights law requires a judicial remedy prior to removal or return. This remedy must consist of an independent and thorough national judicial scrutiny comprising facts and law. Evidence presented by migrants must be taken seriously and examined carefully.

Concluding comment

Migrants have internationally agreed upon human rights. States are under a legal duty to ensure these rights are delivered and respected. All State authorities must ensure that their activities are consistent with their States' international human rights obligations, including as regards migrants. There are three cardinal rules which arise from migrants' human rights:

First, having the nationality of another state does not justify worse treatment by States (or the private sector) than the treatment accorded to citizens.

Secondly, migrants without national immigration documents are human beings with human rights.

Thirdly, the denial of rights, including to migrants, on the basis of colour, religion or other prohibited grounds is wrong and prohibited by international law.

Notes

1   A/71/L.1 para 5.
2   A/71/L.1 para 13.
3   A/71/L.1 para 24.
4   A/71/L.1 para 33.
5   A/71/L.1 para 41.
6   A/71/L.1 para 27.
7   A/71/L.1 para 13.
8   A/71/L.1 para 57.
9   Ibid.
10   A/71/L.1 para 14.
11   A/71/L.1 para 33.

Bibliography

Biersteker, T.J., "State, Sovereignty and Territory," in Carlsnaes et al. (eds.), *Handbook of International Relations*. Thousand Oaks, CA: Sage (2002), 245–272.

Boeles, P.B., *Fair Immigration Proceedings in Europe*. Boston: Martinus Nijhoff (1997).

Boeles, P.B., *Mensen & Papieren: legalisatie en verificatie van bultenlandse documenten in 'probleemlanden'*. Utrecht: FORUM (2003).

Bossuyt, M.J., *Guide to the "Travaux Préparatoires" of the International Covenant on Civil and Political Rights*. Boston: Martinus Nijhoff (1987).

Brett, M., 'The Right to Recognition as a Person before the Law and the Capacity to Act under International Human Rights Law' (2012) *Irish Centre for Human Rights* 9.

Costello, C., 'Human Rights and the Elusive Universal Subject: Immigration Detention under International Human Rights and EU Law' (2012) *Indiana Journal of Global Legal Studies*, 19, 257–303.

Hathaway, J.C., *The Rights of Refugees under International Law*. Cambridge: Cambridge University Press (2005).

Joseph, S., Schultz, J. and Castan, M., *The International Covenant on Civil and Political Rights: Cases, Materials, and Commentary*, 2nd edition. Oxford: Oxford University Press (2004).

Lauterpacht, E. and Bethlehem, D., "The Scope and Content of the Principle of Non-Refoulement: Opinion" in E. Feller, V. Turk and F. Nicholson (eds.), *Refugee Protection in International Law: UNHCR's Global Consultations on International Protection*. Cambridge: Cambridge University Press (2003), 89–90.

Nowak, M., *UN Covenant on Civil and Political Rights: CCPR Commentary*. Germany: N.P. Engel Publisher (2005).

Osborn, P. G., *A Concise Law Dictionary-For Students and Practitioners*. Read Books Ltd, (2013).

Rainey, B., Wicks, E. and Ovey, C., *Jacobs, White and Ovey: The European Convention on Human Rights*. Oxford: Oxford University Press (2014).

Taylor-Nicholson, E. and Oberoi, P., "Background Paper: OHCHR in Cooperation with the GAATW Expert Consultation on Human Rights at International Borders: Exploring Gaps in Policy and Practice", (March 2012).

Van Bueren, G., *The International Law on the Rights of the Child*. Boston: Martinus Nijhoff (1995).

Van Waas, L., *Nationality Matters: Statelessness Under International Law*. Intersentia (2008), 95, 163.

Volio, F., "Legal Personality, Privacy, and the Family," in L. Henkin (ed.), *The International Bill of Rights: The Covenant on Civil and Political Rights*. New York: Columbia University Press (198_), 53–68.

Index

access to territory 9–10
affirmative action to protect-family reunification 68–9
Agiza v Sweden 78–9
arbitrary detention, prohibition of 28–9
arbitrary interference in family life, prohibition of 68
arbitrary removal: effective national procedure against 81–2; prohibition of 44–5
A.S. v Sweden 80
Aung v Canada 80

border, rights at the 21–5, 86; principle of non-discrimination and 21–2; principle of *non-refoulement* and 23–4; protection against collective removal and 24; respect for human dignity and 22–3

CEC v Netherlands 35
children 36–7
Child Rights Convention 55, 69
"civil death" 16–17
collective removal, protection against 24, 44–5
Committee on Economic, Social and Cultural Rights 38
Committee on the Elimination of Racial Discrimination 37, 47
Committee on the Protection of the Rights of All Migrant Workers and Members of Their Families 45
Committee on the Rights of the Child 36–7
conditions, detention 29–30

Convention Against Torture 23–4, 78, 80
Convention on the Elimination of Discrimination Against Women 36–7
courts, fair hearings by impartial 82–3
cultural rights *see* economic, social and cultural rights
C v Australia Communication No. 900/1999 27

detention, immigration 27–30, 87; conditions 29–30; procedural guarantees 29; prohibition of arbitrary detention 28–9
differential treatment, limits to 37–8, 51–3
dignity, human 8–9; respect for 22–3
discrimination: access to territory and 9–10; based on nationality 53–5; dignity and 8–9; principle of non- 21–2; prohibited 51–3; prohibition on hate speech and 76–7; rights and 10–13
domestic workers 63–4

economic, social and cultural rights 50–6, 87–8; discrimination based on nationality and 53–5; prohibited discrimination or difference of treatment 51–3; three categories of obligations 51
expression and opinion, freedom of 74–6, 88–9

fair hearings by impartial courts 82–3
family life and migrants 67–70, 88; prohibition on and protection against

arbitrary interference 68; protection against removal 69–70; requirement of affirmative action to protect-family reunification 68–9; rights to marry and found a family 70
Farag El Dernawi v Libyan Arab Jamahiriya 67, 70
freedom to choose a residence 43

hate speech, prohibition on 76–7
human rights: at the border 21–5, 86; discrimination and 10–13, 51–3; economic, social and cultural 50–6, 87–8; to effective remedy 78–81, 89; fair hearings by impartial courts 82–3; family life and 67–70, 88; freedom of thought, belief and religion and freedom of expression and opinion 72–7, 88–9; in immigration detention 27–30, 87; international commitments to 3–4; of migrants 3–4, 7–8; overview of 3–4, 7–8, 89–90; to recognition 16–19, 86; regardless of status 36–7, 87; in residence and removal 42–8, 87; at work 58–64, 88
Human Rights Council 47

Ibrahima Gueye et al. v France, Human Rights Committee 50
Ilyasov v Kazakhstan Human Rights Committee 42
immigration detention 27–30, 87; conditions 29–30; procedural guarantees 29; prohibition of arbitrary detention 28–9
International Convention on the Elimination of All Forms of Racial Discrimination 46
international human rights law 59–61
International labour law 61
International Labour Organization (ILO) 61; Migrant Workers Convention of 1949 61–2; Migrant Workers Convention of 1975 62–3
irregular status 35–9, 87; human rights regardless of status and 37–8; legally compliant migration management 38–9

Jansen-Gielen v the Netherlands 82

Ke Chun Rong v Australia 80

language 53
legally compliant migration management 38–9
liberty of movement, right to 43

Madafferi v Australia 69–70
Mansour Ahani v Canada 81–2
marriage rights 70
migrants: economic, social and cultural rights of 50–6, 87–8; family life and 67–70, 88; freedom of thought, belief and religion and freedom of expression and opinion 72–7, 88–9; immigration detention of 27–30, 87; irregular status of 35–9, 87; overview of human rights of 3–4, 7–8, 89–90; residence and removal rights 42–8, 87; rights at the border 21–5, 86; rights at work 58–64, 88; right to effective remedy 78–81, 89; right to fair hearings by impartial courts 82–3; right to recognition 16–19, 86; UN Declaration for Migrants and Refugees 1–2, 85
migration management, legally compliant 38–9

nationality, discrimination based on 53–5
New York Declaration for Migrants and Refugees 1–2, 5, 85; on dignity, discrimination or differential treatment 8–9; on discrimination and access to territory 9–10; on discrimination and rights 10–13; on economic, social and cultural rights of migrants 50, 87–8; on family life and migrants 67–70, 88; on freedom of thought, belief and religion and freedom of expression and opinion 72, 88–9; on immigration detention 27, 87; on irregular status 35, 87; on rights at the border 21, 86; on rights at work 58, 88; on rights of residence and in removal 42; on right to effective remedy 78, 89; on right to recognition 16, 86
Ngambi and Nebol v France 69
Nirmal Singh v Canada 80

non-discrimination, principle of 21–2, 47
non-refoulement, principle of 23–4,
  47–8, 79–80

*Opinion No. 28/2016 concerning
  Nazanin Zaghari-Ratcliffe* 21

Pillai and Joachimpillai v Canada 79
procedural guarantees and detention 29

race 52–3
recognition, right to 16–19, 86; how
  migrants prove they are a human
  with 18–19; before the law 18;
  prohibiting "civil death" and 16–17;
  scope of 17–18
refugees, UN Declaration for Migrants
  and Refugees and 1–2; *see also*
  migrants
religion 53
remedy, right to effective 78–81, 89
removal: effective national procedure
  against arbitrary 81–2; family
  life and protection against 69–70;
  prohibition of arbitrary and
  collective 24, 44–5; rights 42–8, 87
residence rights 42–8, 87; prohibition
  of arbitrary and collective removal
  44–5; right to leave any country and
  to return to his or her country 46–7;
  right to liberty of movement and
  freedom to choose residence 43
reunification, family 68–9

social rights *see* economic, social and
  cultural rights
Social Rights Covenant *see* economic,
  social and cultural rights
Sogi v Canada 81–2
Special Rapporteur on the Human
  Rights of Migrants 35–6
status, irregular 35–9, 87

thought, belief and religion, freedom of
  72–4, 88–9

United Nations 1–2 *see* New York
  Declaration for Migrants and
  Refugees
Universal Declaration for Human
  Rights 1–2

Vienna Law on Treaties 54

women 36–7
work, rights at 58–64, 88; domestic
  workers and 63–4; ILO Migrant
  Workers Convention of 1949 61–2;
  ILO Migrant Workers Convention
  of 1975 62–3; international human
  rights law and 59–61; International
  labour law and 61

X.H.L. v the Netherlands 79

Yilmaz-Dogan v the Netherlands 58